IMAGES
of America

GREATER
SYRACUSE
A TWENTIETH-CENTURY ALBUM

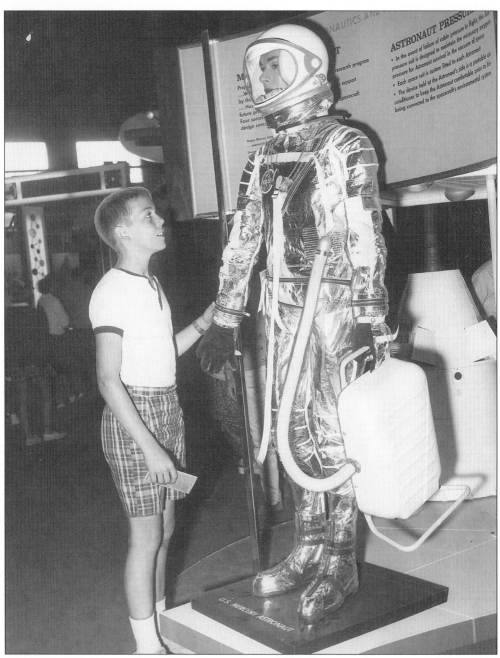

ASTRONAUT DISPLAY AT NEW YORK STATE FAIR, 1964. America's first manned space flights, under the Mercury Program, were recent successes when this exhibit opened. The first seven Mercury astronauts became new heroes to a young generation of Central New York baby boomers.

IMAGES
of America

GREATER
SYRACUSE
A TWENTIETH-CENTURY ALBUM

Onondaga Historical Association
Text by Dennis J. Connors

ARCADIA

Published by Arcadia Publishing,
an imprint of Tempus Publishing, Inc.
2 Cumberland Street
Charleston, SC 29401

Printed in Great Britain.

Library of Congress Catalog Card Number applied for.

For all general information contact Arcadia Publishing at:
Telephone 843-853-2070
Fax 843-853-0044
E-Mail arcadia@charleston.net

For customer service and orders:
Toll-Free 1-888-313-BOOK

Visit us on the internet at http://www.arcadiaimages.com

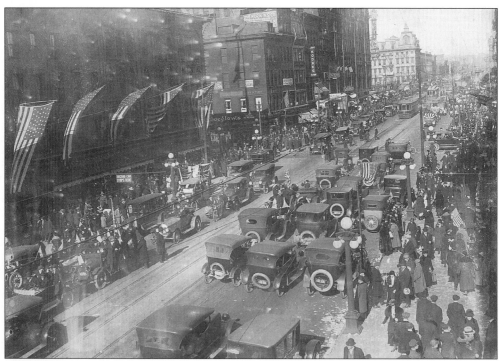

DOWNTOWN SYRACUSE CELEBRATION, C. 1918. This image may show the reaction in Syracuse upon hearing of the November 11, 1918 armistice that ended World War I. Throughout the 19th and 20th centuries, downtown has served as the symbolic center of the Greater Syracuse community. It has been a shared place, over many eras, that has served to provide unifying experiences for diverse populations and geographic sectors of our county. Hopefully, that critical function will continue throughout the next century.

4

CONTENTS

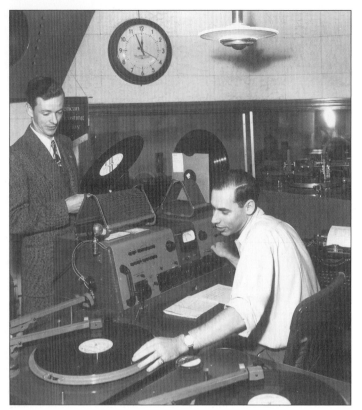

WAGE RADIO CONTROL ROOM, 1946. With television not yet available, radio ruled as the great communication medium of the 1930s and 1940s. The studios of WAGE were located on the fifth floor of the Loew Building on West Jefferson Street. The engineers, pictured at left, are Robert Ardner (left) and Howard Ialberg.

INTRODUCTION

The turn of a century is a rare event. It has only happened twice since our nation was formed. For most of us, the arrival of the 21st century is the only one we will ever experience. It becomes, therefore, a special moment for our community to consider the passage of time. How have we progressed? What has changed? How has the human condition remained the same? What might we have done different or better?

We can fondly remember good times, laugh at striking changes, or admire sacrifices and achievements. A community's past should also be broadly shared. It can help unify people across generational, ethnic, and geographical differences.

For almost 140 years, the Onondaga Historical Association has been serving as the primary repository for the history and memories of Syracuse and Onondaga County. Some of the richest resources under its care are the tens of thousands of photographic images in its collection. These create extraordinary windows into the past. The advent of the year 2000 seemed an appropriate occasion to utilize these resources to assemble a visual, 20th-century portfolio of Greater Syracuse. This volume is the result.

This book is not a comprehensive history of the last 100 years. That is not its intent. The chosen images are not measures of the most famous people or significant events. The volume functions more as a scrapbook, offering glimpses into our past—for some, a way to share memories and experiences; for others, a chance to gain new insights about the community.

The book is organized into six chapters, each defined by a specific period from 1900 to 1999. While all the images are local scenes, the captions often seek to tie the subject into a national context. The evolution of the Syracuse area has its own distinct character but was always shaped by trends, fashions, and policies that existed on a broader scale, impacting how we identify our lives. The dividing points are not regular and even, but they reflect the fact that history evolves in irregular and sometimes dramatic ways.

The interval of CHAPTER 1, 1900 TO 1919, acknowledges that the first two decades of the century saw a continuation of several, late-19th-century attitudes and styles. Women's fashions still reached the ground. Many believed that voting should remain a male privilege. Horse-drawn vehicles continued in common use. Solar salt-evaporating sheds still hugged the Onondaga Lake shoreline. The Erie Canal remained a fixture of Syracuse's Clinton Square, as it had for most of the 1800s. Beyond Syracuse, surrounding towns and villages looked much like they had during the 1880s and 1890s.

But the first 20 years of this century were also marked by defining changes. The automobile arrived and grew in influence. Airplane flight became a reality. Immigration from eastern and southern Europe soared. The joint arrival of Colonial Revival, as well as the Arts-and-Crafts style, offered alternatives to the Victorian decorative excesses of the previous century. Electricity spread throughout cities like Syracuse. The period's close was underlined by the dual adversity of America's entry into the trenches of World War I in 1917 and an even more deadly influenza epidemic in 1919.

CHAPTER 2, 1920 TO 1929, recognizes that this decade witnessed radical departures from the previous two. It began with the era of Prohibition—a bold national experiment to ban the production and sale of intoxicating beverages. More significantly, 1920 also saw the granting of nationwide voting rights to women. During the era, female fashions exhibited new freedoms, mirroring the vitality and exuberance of the times. Hollywood movie-making escalated, leading to the construction of awe-inspiring movie palaces in Syracuse and across America. The stock market soared. Syracuse's Franklin auto company became the area's largest employer. The Erie and Oswego Canals disappeared and were replaced by automobile boulevards. By the late 1920s, the arrival of Art Deco styling gave the decade a flashy new look. However, optimism came to a crashing halt in 1929 with the collapse of the stock market and the arrival of a massive economic depression.

The period of CHAPTER 3, 1930 TO 1947, is defined by two major events that shaped the life of an entire generation: the Great Depression and World War II. Life went on during the 1930s. People shopped, went to the movies, rode the trolley, attended school, or took in a ball game. For most, however, it was also a very challenging decade. In Syracuse, as elsewhere, thousands were out of a job or working reduced hours. Finances were stretched everywhere, in personal households, in business, and in government. Some institutions, like Syracuse's huge Franklin factory, went bankrupt, but the community looked to the future. Relocation of the city's grade-level railroad tracks, a major undertaking, was completed. Onondaga Lake Park was opened. A new baseball franchise arrived, and a local team won the first American Hockey League championship trophy.

By 1941, the economy had not fully recovered, but people were hopeful. World War II quickly changed everyone's perspective. Sacrifices would need to continue, but with a new emphasis. Greater Syracuse and the nation responded. Men went to fight and die, others turned industry into a powerful machine for war, and everybody celebrated when the fighting ended. But it took a year or two for the now prosperous nation to regain its consumer-driven focus. When it did, by the late 1940s, the community and the nation boldly entered a new era of affluence and change.

CHAPTER 4, 1948 TO 1963, explores Onondaga County in a period when television became a medium that altered lifestyles and viewpoints. The 1950s saw the move to the suburbs begin as Syracuse's population dropped for the first time. America began to launch satellites, and then people, into space. Rock and roll could be found on the dials of radio stations and at gymnasium record hops. Shopping plazas sprouted northeast and west of the city. The region enjoyed a golden era in sports, with the holder of a national boxing title, a collegiate football powerhouse, and an NBA championship team calling the Syracuse area home. The ornate, 19th-century look of the city was no longer seen as a symbol of prosperity but a sign of aging, needing to be replaced. Elaborately detailed mansions on James Street began to be swept away for fresh, spare office structures.

The 1960s started with the election of a charismatic new president, the first born in the 20th century. Despite the growing visibility of civil rights injustices and the shadow of the Cold War, Syracuse, Onondaga County, and the nation looked forward to their best years ever. But in 1963, a tragic rifle shot in Dallas became a milestone and turning point in the life of the nation.

CHAPTER 5, 1964 TO 1974, covers a relatively brief span, but one that marks a growing, often radical rejection of the status quo. It was a period marked by excesses. Anti-Vietnam War protests escalated to an eruption point with soldiers firing on students at Kent State. Block after block of downtown streets and older neighborhoods were leveled flat in the name of urban renewal. The bottom of pants flared to conspicuous widths, and women's skirts climbed to remarkable heights. But the nation also made a recommitment to civil rights for everyone and placed a man on the moon. Residents of Central New York State experienced all of this and more. Giant expressways were carved through Syracuse, a dynamic mayor named Lee Alexander reigned supreme in his first term in Syracuse City Hall, and a hamburger cost 15¢. The departure of U.S. troops from Vietnam in 1973 and the resignation of President Nixon in 1974 marked points for new national directions.

Defining the last period, CHAPTER 6, 1975 TO 1999, was a bit easier. We are, perhaps, still too close in time to these years to clearly delineate all the trends and benchmarks. There is the computer revolution, the continuing progress of women into traditional male bastions, the struggle to find ways to revitalize our urban cores, and new community projects like the renovated Burnet Park Zoo and Mulroy Civic Center. However, the last quarter of the century is primarily this: the period that puts closure on a century of vast transformations, challenges, and accomplishments.

The diversity and magnitude of the Onondaga Historical Association's photographic holdings are the result of support from many individuals and institutions. In the preparation of this volume, the commitment of the Syracuse newspapers in donating thousands of images to the collection, over many years, has been invaluable. The remarkable work of their many talented photographers has created a tremendous legacy for this community. This book also benefited from the foresight of Robert Arnold, a local commercial photographer, whose firm began in the early 20th century. Arnold's decision in 1976 to donate his accumulation of more than 7,000 negatives to the Onondaga Historical Association created a significant resource. Additionally, the vision of Syracuse photojournalist Carl Single's family, in gifting his body of work to the historical association after his untimely death in 1996, must be acknowledged in assembling this album.

I also wish to thank Judy Haven, the historical association's research coordinator, for her assistance. This book would also not have been possible without the support of the association's members, donors, staff, and board who, together, maintain this organization in the forefront of preserving the vibrant heritage of Syracuse and Onondaga County. A visit to its downtown Syracuse museum is encouraged, as it offers a unique journey through time for all to enjoy.

Dennis J. Connors
Syracuse, New York
July 1999

One

1900–1919

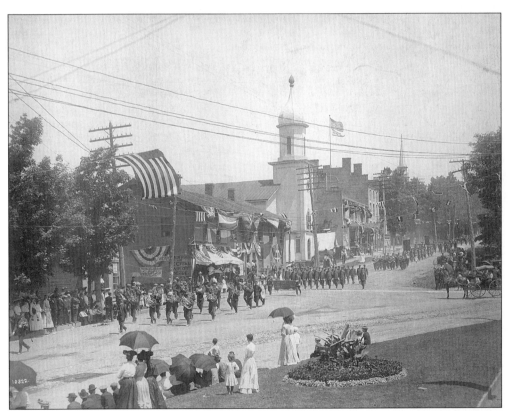

FIREMEN'S PARADE IN MANLIUS, C. 1904. This view, looking east up Seneca Street, shows the Marcellus Union Fire Department passing. The many fire departments of Onondaga County's towns and villages have long been a point of pride and identity for their various communities. This event likely occurred on a warm summer day, judging by the women's white outfits, the numerous umbrellas for shade, and the "ice cream for sale here" banner.

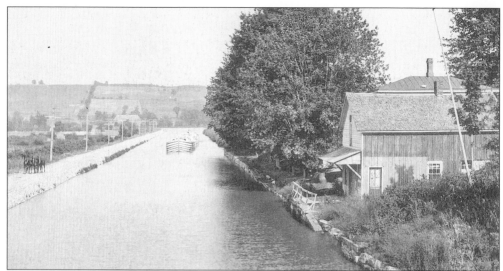

ERIE CANAL SCENE, C. 1900. This view, taken from the Burdick Road Bridge near Fayetteville, shows a canal barge heading west toward Syracuse. In the beginning of the 20th century, the old Erie Canal was still being used, but it had long been eclipsed as a leading shipping route by the many railroads that crisscrossed the state. Within 20 years, it would be abandoned and replaced by the state Barge Canal.

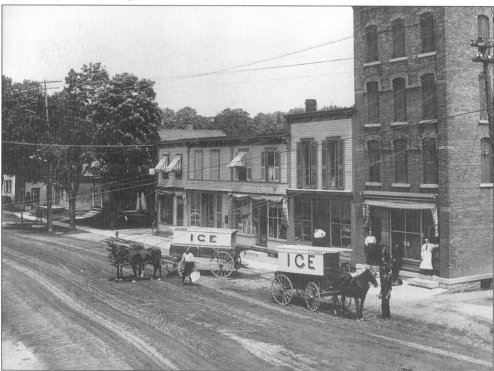

ICE WAGONS ON JORDAN STREET IN SKANEATELES, 1908. During the early decades of the 20th century, before widespread distribution of electrical power and related appliances, keeping perishable food cool was dependent on an icebox and regular ice deliveries. Ice was cut from frozen area lakes in winter and carefully stored by suppliers until needed.

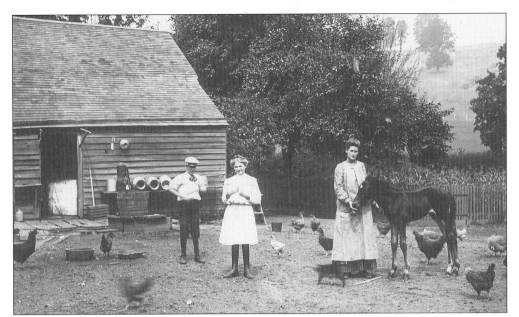

Farm Yard in the Town of Onondaga, c. 1908. Farming has always been, and remains, an important part of Onondaga County's economy and lifestyle. A greater percentage of the local population experienced rural life during the first two decades of the 20th century than they do at the century's close.

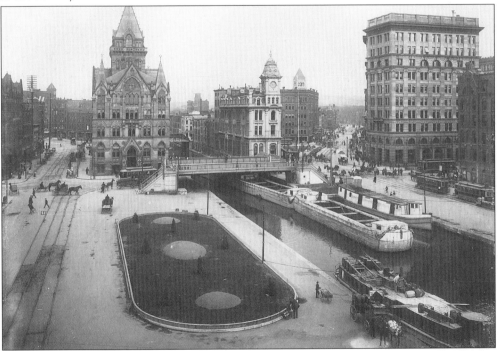

Clinton Square, c. 1905. As the 20th century began, the population of Syracuse was 108,374 and growing. Sixty-four percent of the county population lived in the city. It was the bustling hub of the region. The architectural landmarks of Clinton Square's east side have provided a dramatic link to our predecessors over the entire span of the century.

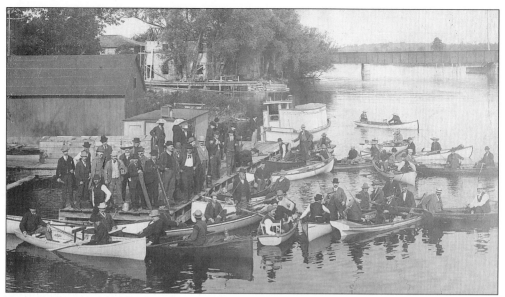

FISHING OUTING ON ONEIDA RIVER AT BREWERTON, C. 1900. Oneida Lake has long been known for its fine fishing. This group of sportsmen head out to enjoy the ageless pastime, although their dress is decidedly more formal than the style worn by today's anglers. Note the small passenger launch tied up at the dock.

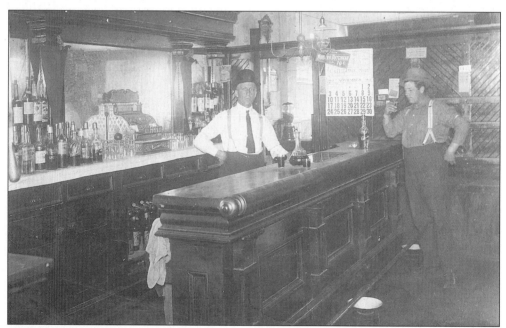

WEBSTER HOUSE BAR IN CICERO, 1912. Throughout America, the local tavern increasingly became a fixture in area villages and neighborhoods during the 19th century. Hundreds populated Syracuse and Onondaga County by the beginning of the 20th century, much to the dismay of those who saw it as a source of many evils. These "prohibitionists" would succeed in temporarily outlawing the sale of liquor by 1920.

12

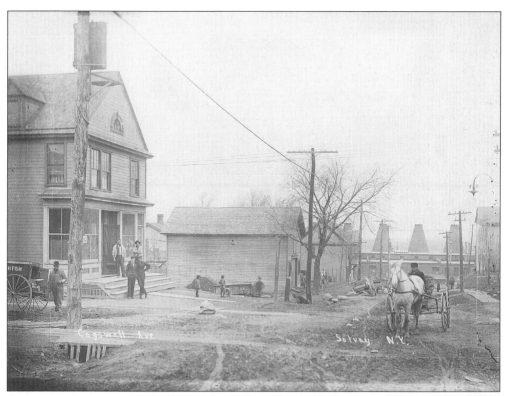

COGSWELL AVENUE IN SOLVAY, C. 1900. The village of Solvay grew up around the Solvay Process Company and other industries in the late 19th century. In the distance, beyond Milton Avenue, are the "bottle" kilns of the Iroquois China Company.

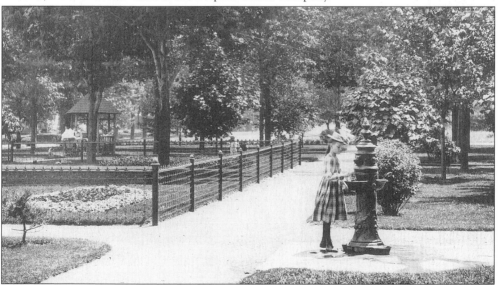

WASHINGTON SQUARE, C. 1900. In the early 20th century, smaller cities like Syracuse saw an expansion of the formal park landscaping style that had developed in larger cities during the late 19th century. The original village green for the village of Salina had become an elegant north side retreat by 1900. Today, it is a simple playground known as Washington Park.

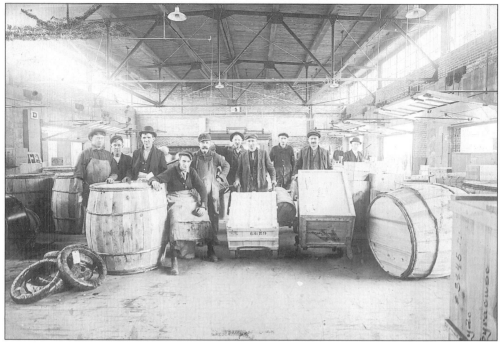

DL&W RAILROAD FREIGHT HOUSE WORKERS, C. 1902. In the early years of the 20th century, railroads reigned supreme for the shipment of most goods. Railroad tracks crisscrossed the city and county, with many sidings built adjacent to manufacturing sites. Each railroad had its own freight houses, where a variety of goods for businesses and individuals moved in and out regularly on the many daily trains.

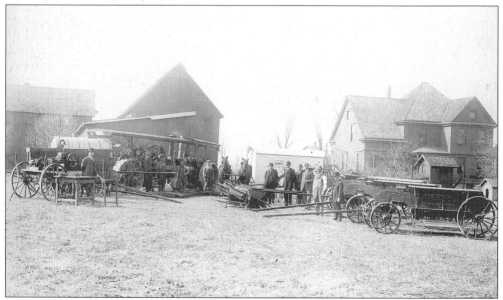

TOWN OF DEWITT HIGHWAY DEPARTMENT, 1908. The 19th-century technology of steam-powered tractors and horse-drawn wagons still dominated the town's available equipment in the early 20th century. Eventually, trucks powered by the modern gasoline combustion engine would replace both.

THE 300 BLOCK OF SOUTH SALINA STREET, 1912. Possibly festooned for a July 4 celebration, it was not unusual for the sidewalks of downtown Syracuse's shopping district to be packed during this era. The combination of stores and services that it equaled at the time were simply unmatched anywhere else in the region. Short pants, called "knickers," were standard fare for young boys, and in warm weather, summer white was common for ladies.

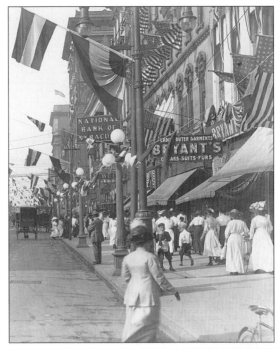

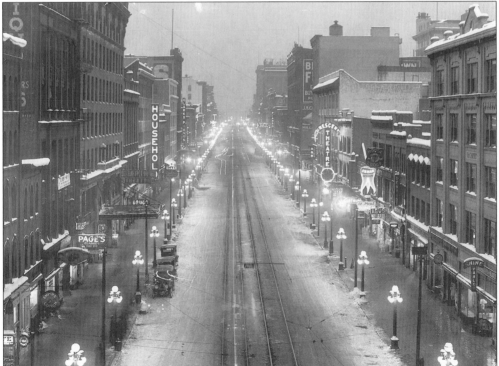

VIEW NORTH ON SALINA STREET AT NIGHT, 1914. Widespread distribution of exterior electric lighting was a new development during the first decades of the 20th century. Its use for signs and streetlights dramatically changed the nighttime look of American cities, like Syracuse.

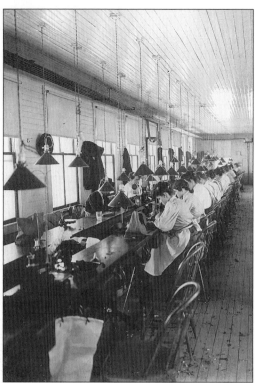

MANLIUS GLOVE FACTORY, C. 1905. Single women had become a growing part of the workforce in the 19th century and were often assigned to tasks that were believed to require detail and dexterity. Although they comprised an increasingly vital part of the economy, women still could not vote until 1920.

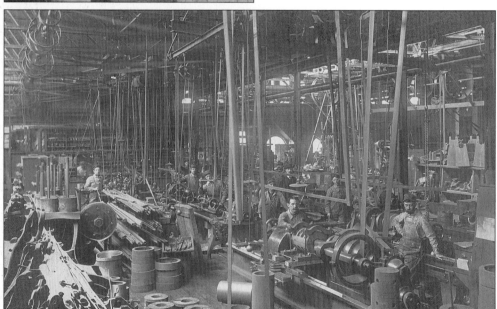

STRAIGHT LINE ENGINE WORKS, C. 1900. Started on Syracuse's west end in 1880, this firm is an example of the significant heavy manufacturing profile that Syracuse's economy achieved by the early 20th century. Straight Line built steam engines used throughout the world to power electric generators. It closed in 1961, and the site on South Geddes Street is now a small shopping plaza. These production machines were powered by numerous belts, driven by the spinning shafts and wheels overhead.

UNLOADING COAL AT MEMPHIS, C. 1900. Communities that had grown up at the edge of the old Erie Canal continued to depend on it as a practical route for shipping bulky cargoes during the first two decades of the 20th century. However, mule-powered barges were outdated technology. By 1919, the State Barge Canal allowed faster and more efficient tugboats to pull larger barges, and the old Erie was abandoned.

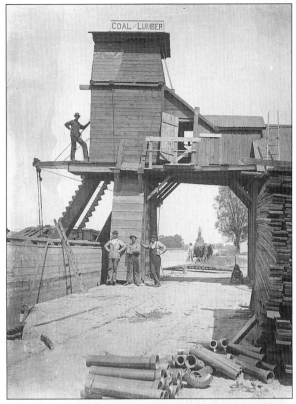

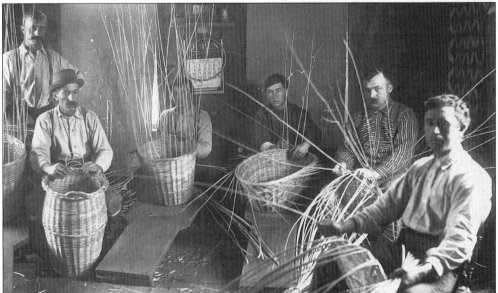

GEORGE FISCHER'S WILLOW BASKET SHOP IN LIVERPOOL, 1901. This cottage industry began in Liverpool during the mid-19th century, exploiting the common willow shoots found growing in the nearby Onondaga Lake shore area. It continued into the first decades of the 20th century, but the local hand-made craft would be replaced by inexpensive imports and other materials.

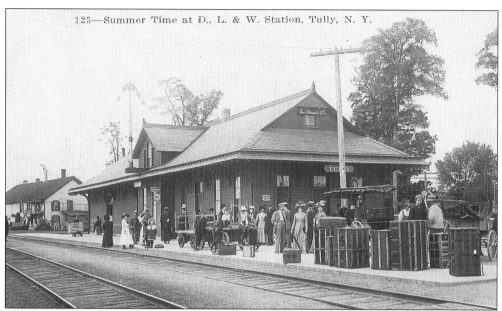

125—Summer Time at D., L. & W. Station, Tully, N. Y.

DELAWARE, LACKAWANNA & WESTERN RAILROAD STATION IN TULLY, C. 1905. Several small communities in Onondaga County could boast of having their own passenger railroad station at the beginning of the 20th century. During the summer, the one in Tully was also used by vacationers heading to some of the Tully Lake cottages or hotels that existed at the time.

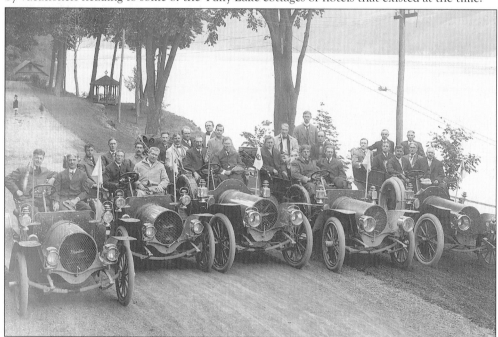

FRANKLIN AUTOMOBILES ALONG SKANEATELES LAKE, 1907. The automobile arrived in Onondaga County and much of America with the dawn of the 20th century; however, it would be a few years before mass production made it affordable for the majority of people. At first, many cities had auto manufacturers. The Franklin was produced in Syracuse from 1902 until 1934. John Wilkinson, its inventor, is driving the second vehicle from the right.

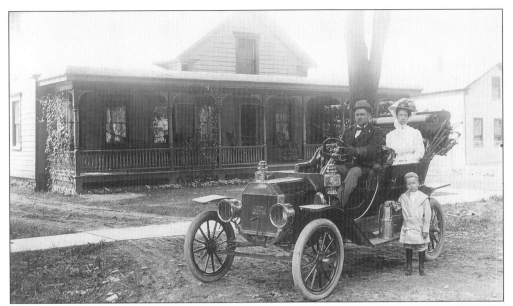

MODEL T FORD ON PINE STREET IN JORDAN, C. 1910. Henry Ford's Model T began to dominate the automobile market when it was introduced in 1908. His start of mass, assembly line production in 1913 brought the Model T's price down, and demand soared. Proud new owners posed with their Model Ts across America. By 1920, Americans were increasingly adapting their lifestyles and the look of their communities to suit the influence of the automobile.

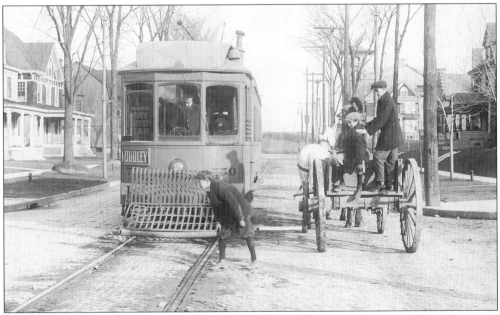

SYRACUSE ELECTRIC RAILWAY CAR AT EUCLID NEAR WESTCOTT STREET, 1913. This posed photo is part of a "safety" series intended to illustrate the potential for accidents involving streetcars. Electric street railways helped allow the development of new, outlying neighborhoods in the first two decades of the 20th century and served as the city's primary mass transit system through the 1930s.

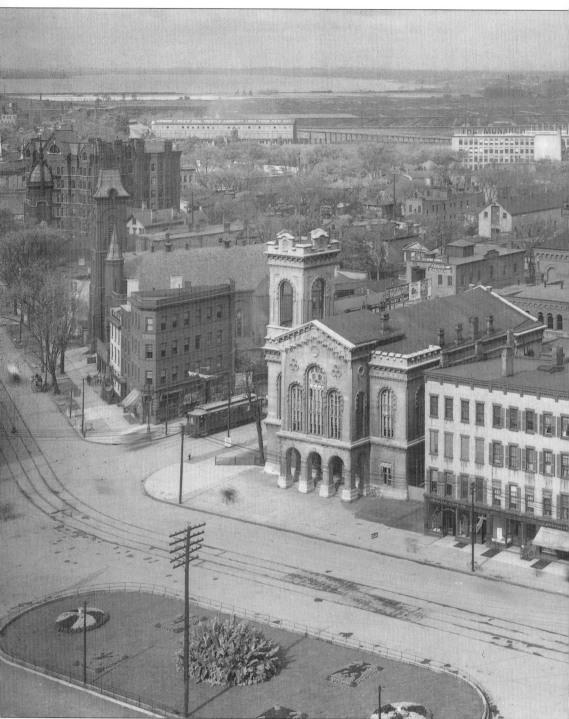

VIEW FROM CLINTON SQUARE, NORTH TO ONONDAGA LAKE, 1903. At the beginning of the 20th century, Syracuse was a growing city that would continue to expand its physical boundaries through the 1920s. Although the remnants of the salt industry were still visible in the distance, it was a fading part of the economy. It had been replaced by a great diversity of

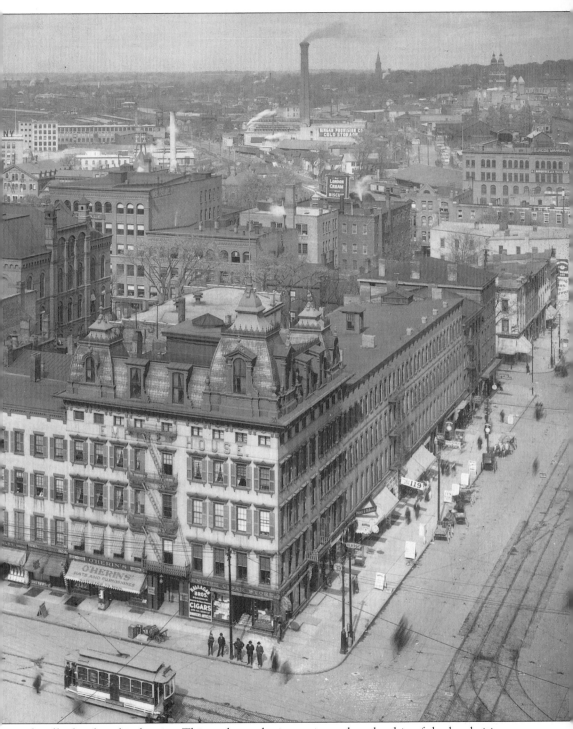

locally developed industries. This spoke to the ingenuity and work ethic of the local citizenry, whose composition was bolstered by the ongoing arrival of immigrants in the early 20th century, primarily from eastern and southern Europe.

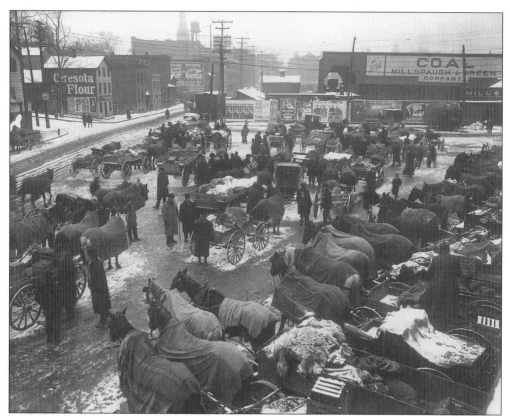

NORTH SIDE MARKET, 1910. In the 19th century, Clinton Square had functioned as the location for farmers to sell their produce to city residents. As the 20th century brought more formal landscaping to the square, the market shifted north to this site. The intersection of Belden and Pearl Streets (left) is the 1999 location of Syracuse's famous Columbus Bakery.

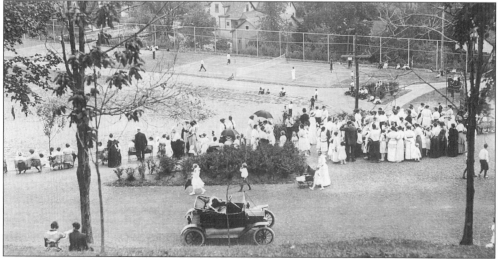

LINCOLN PARK, 1914. Syracuse actively developed its young municipal park system in the first decades of the 20th century. In the northeast district of the city on a warm August day, spectators enjoyed a tennis match and what may be a baseball game (left).

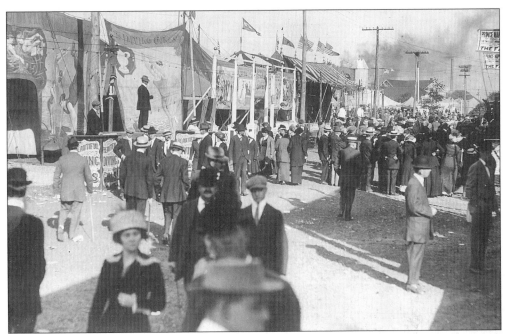

NEW YORK STATE FAIR, 1913. Throughout the 20th century, residents of Syracuse and Onondaga County have had the special opportunity to look forward to this annual end-of-summer ritual that happened right in their community. In 1913, visitors dressed more formally than now, as they contemplated paying 10¢ to see "Beautiful Diving Girls" or "Prince Napoleon—The Smallest Midget on Earth" at the midway sideshow.

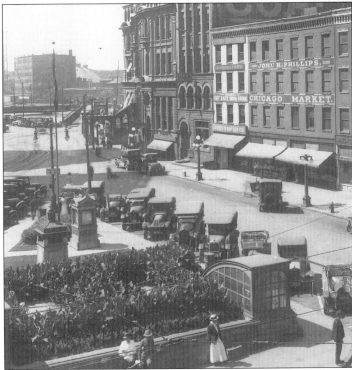

HANOVER SQUARE, C. 1918. By the end of the 20th century's second decade, the presence of the automobile created parking issues in downtown Syracuse. This formally landscaped park, located in one of the city's oldest public spaces, also featured underground public rest rooms, accessible by the glass enclosed stairways.

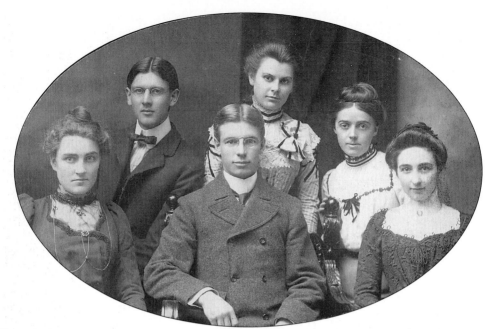

JAMESVILLE HIGH SCHOOL FACULTY, 1901. The late 19th and early 20th centuries saw a rapid increase in the percentage of America's children that regularly attended school. The national percentage of adolescents in high school doubled from 1890 to 1910, although it only reached 32% by 1920. Levels were higher in New York State, where compulsory education had long been in effect.

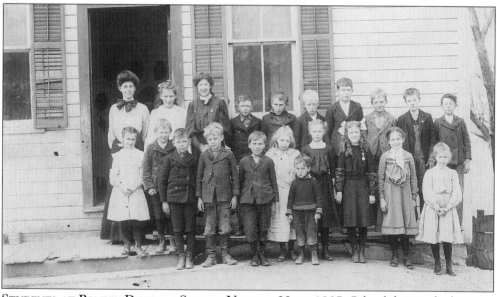

STUDENTS AT POMPEY DISTRICT SCHOOL NUMBER 22, C. 1907. School districts had not yet consolidated in much of the county, and numerous small school buildings dotted the countryside during the early decades of the 20th century. The innocent faces on these students from the Oran area cannot reflect what we know—that they will soon grow up to face World War I, the Great Depression, and the emotion of seeing their children's generation fight World War II.

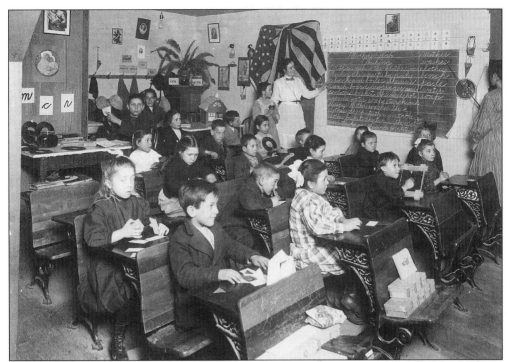

BOYD SCHOOL IN SOLVAY, 1918. Elementary school students work on what appears to be a vocabulary lesson. The content is also a clear reflection of the times. The paragraph on the chalkboard is titled, "Mother's Work—Washing." The list of needed supplies—pails, tubs, boiler, bench, washboard, wringer, soap, starch, bluing, and a clothesline—explains why washing clothes in 1918 was a tedious, all-day affair.

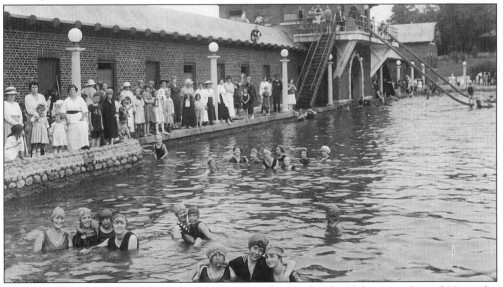

BATHING POOL AT ONONDAGA PARK, C.1917. The south side of the reconfigured Hiawatha Lake was reserved for females in the early years of the 20th century. This reflected the continuing morals of the 19th century, where social customs of the Victorian age dictated a much greater degree of separation between sexes and their defined roles in life.

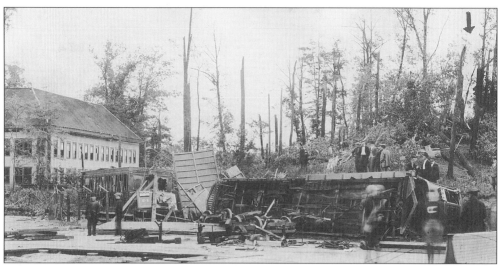

TORNADO DAMAGE AT LONG BRANCH PARK, 1912. The 1890s and early 20th century was the great era of Onondaga Lake's resorts and amusement parks. Several flourished until World War I, serviced by interurban electric railway lines. On September 15, 1912, a freak tornado touched down in the middle of one resort, tossing trolley cars, killing a motorman, and devastating the landscape. It remains a local weather milestone of the 20th century.

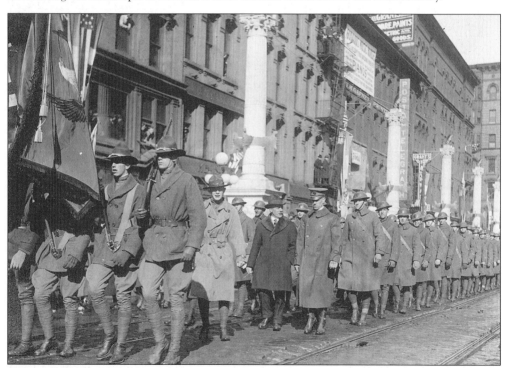

PARADE OF WORLD WAR I SOLDIERS, 1919. An elaborate colonnade decorated Syracuse's Vanderbilt Square as citizens celebrated the return of local units. Approximately 12,000 men from Onondaga County served among the over one million doughboys sent from America. The brutality of this foreign war sent Central New Yorkers and other Americans into a period of isolationism, avoiding interest in the affairs of other nations.

Two
1920–1929

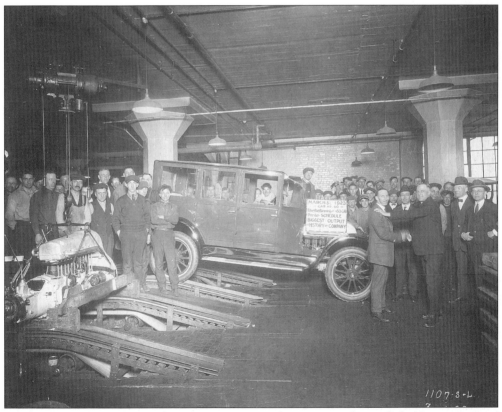

FRANKLIN FACTORY, 1923. The 1920s was an era of optimism and growth for the community. Local industries, like Syracuse's Franklin auto plant, employed thousands and looked toward continuing expansion. The robust economy fueled new home construction in outer city neighborhoods like Eastwood, Strathmore, and Scottholm.

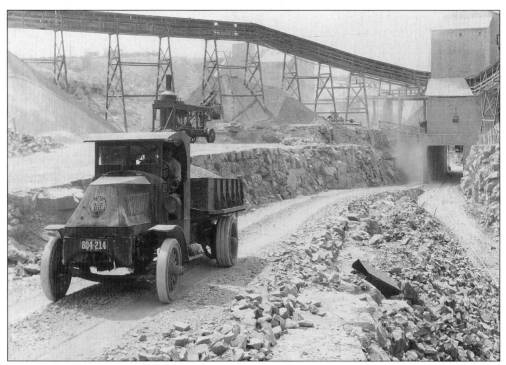

JAMESVILLE QUARRY, 1921. The massive Solvay Process plant, established in Geddes in 1881, required huge quantities of area limestone for its chemical production of soda ash. In 1912, it opened a new quarry operation, just east of Jamesville, where this Mack truck was employed.

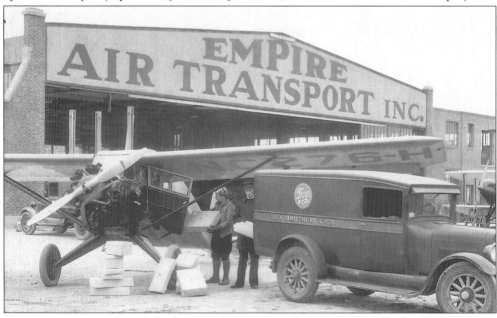

AMBOY AIRPORT, C. 1929. In the years before the end of World War II, the Syracuse area's major municipal airport was located in Amboy. It was where regular airline service to the area started. At a commercial hanger, packages are loaded for Dey Brothers, one of Syracuse's large downtown department stores.

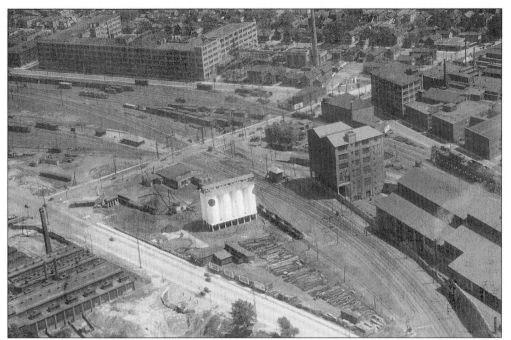

ERIE BOULEVARD WEST AND GEDDES STREET, C. 1929. The near west end of Syracuse developed in the late 19th and early 20th centuries as a neighborhood of heavy industry. This was aided, in part, by easy access to the DL&W railroad line, whose yards are visible at the upper left. At the time, an auto on Geddes Street had to pass over nearly ten sets of tracks, none with grade crossing gates.

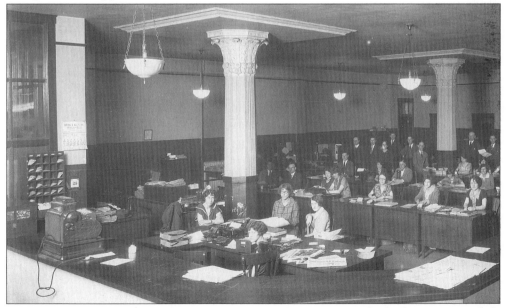

SYRACUSE JOURNAL ADVERTISING OFFICE, 1925. Syracuse had three major daily newspapers in the 1920s. The *Journal* was founded in 1839 but would be bought and merged with the *Herald* in 1939. Women workers seen here wear the short hairstyles that were popular in the 1920s.

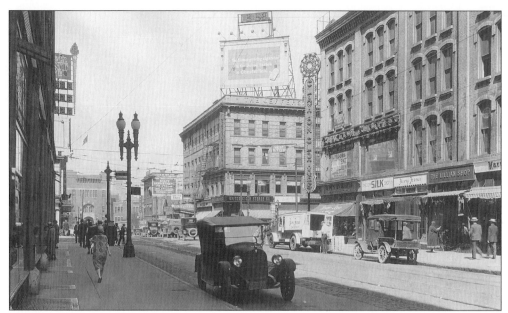

JEFFERSON STREET LOOKING WEST ACROSS SALINA STREET, 1925. This bustling shopping area featured stores that were at a second tier to the main retailers with storefronts on Salina Street. Fanny Farmer Candies, seen here receiving a delivery, has had a retail presence in downtown Syracuse for most of the 20th century.

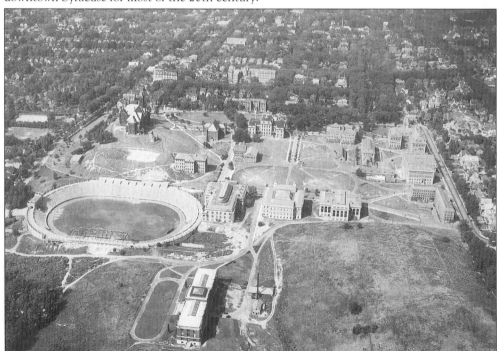

SYRACUSE UNIVERSITY CAMPUS, C. 1924. The university experienced a sizable building boom in the early 20th century under Chancellor James Roscoe Day, adding a standard neo-classical quad of buildings to its original row of Victorian landmarks. The first building of the Forestry School campus, Bray Hall, is also visible at the bottom.

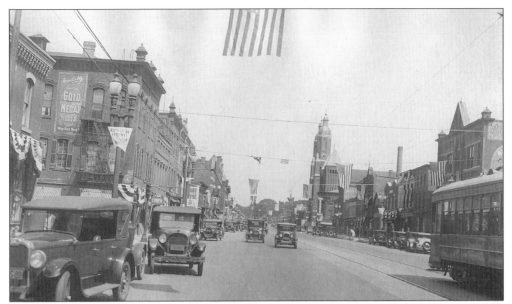

NORTH SALINA STREET FROM DIVISION STREET, 1927. In the early 19th century, North Salina Street had been the road that connected the villages of Salina and Syracuse. It functioned as a commercial artery throughout both the 19th and 20th centuries, first with a German flavor and later with an Italian flair, as it passed through the heart of those ethnic communities.

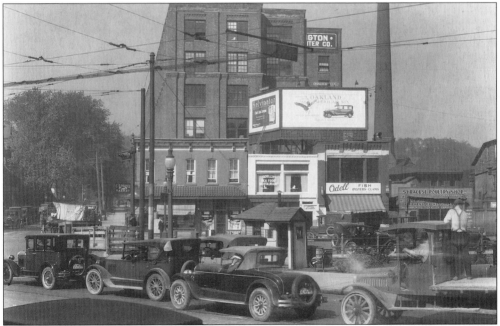

INTERSECTION OF SOUTH CLINTON, WEST ONONDAGA, AND GIFFORD STREETS, c. 1928. This busy scene captures the pace and pattern of life in the 1920s and early 1930s. Beyond looms the large Remington Typewriter factory. The small shack (center) is for the railroad crossing guard. The tracks of the DL&W railroad crossed West Onondaga just in front of the driver (left).

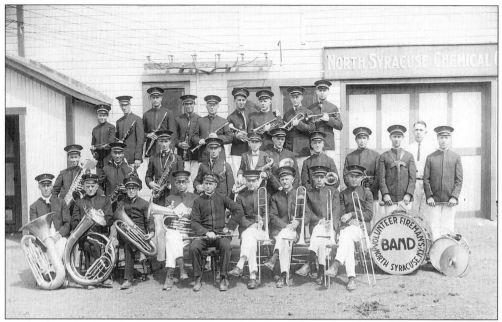

NORTH SYRACUSE VOLUNTEER FIREMAN'S BAND, 1924. At a national level, John Philip Sousa and his band popularized patriotic marches at the turn of the 20th century. Community celebrations, flag-waving parades, and summer concerts afforded opportunities throughout Onondaga County in the early 20th century for local counterparts to present his rousing music.

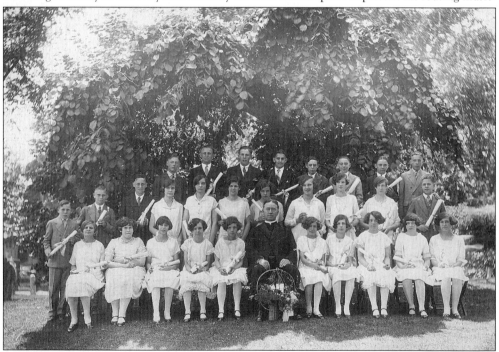

ST. JOHN THE BAPTIST GRAMMAR SCHOOL CLASS, 1926. Monsignor Charles McEvoy poses with the school's first graduating class, probably 8th graders. The students' names reflect the 19th century German and Irish heritage of the north side.

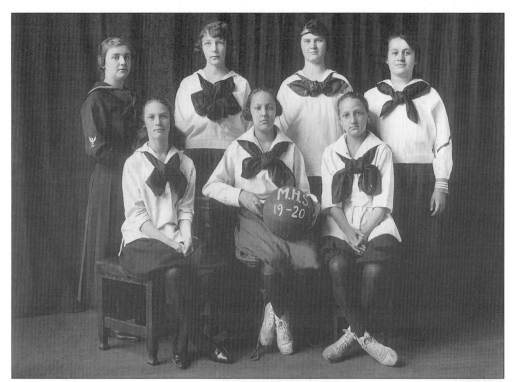

MANLIUS HIGH SCHOOL FEMALE BASKETBALL TEAM, 1920. Basketball developed in the 1890s and became popular in the early 20th century. Female teams were soon participating, but women's rules were different than men's at the time, with the former designed to prevent rough play and limit physical exertion.

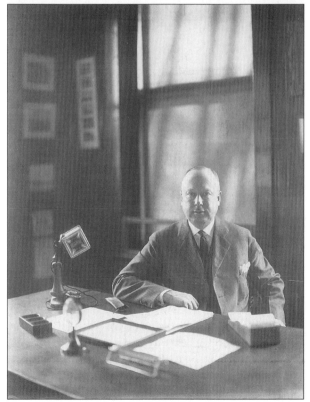

BURNS LYMAN SMITH, C. 1929. The son of typewriter manufacturer, Lyman C. Smith, Burns was a successful businessman in his own right. He was an officer in the family typewriter firm and headed the Syracuse Malleable Iron Works. It produced one of America's most successful lines of truck and auto wheels, employing over 1,000 workers at its North Geddes Street plant in the 1920s. He died in 1941.

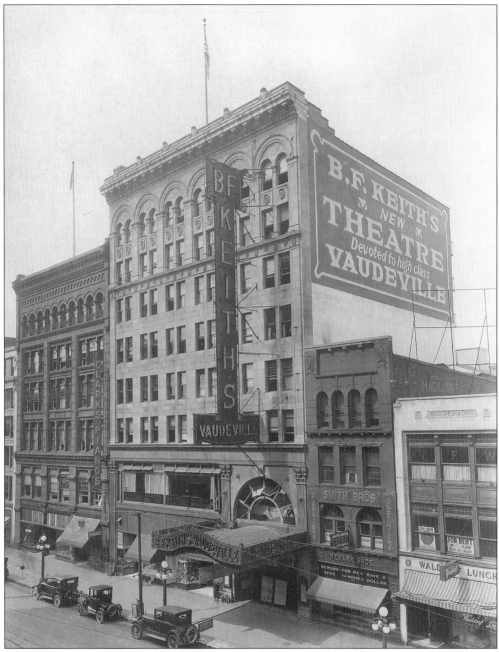

B.F. KEITH'S VAUDEVILLE THEATER, C. 1921. Although large playhouses existed in Syracuse earlier, the 1920s mark the era of the grand theater palaces. Keith's opened in the 400 block of South Salina Street in 1920. It featured both movies and live vaudeville acts on stage.

INTERIOR OF KEITH'S, C. 1929.
B.F. Keith's ornate classical-style interior contrasted with its later rival, Loew's State (now Landmark Theater), which featured a more ornate Persian theme. Keith's was demolished in 1967 as part of the urban renewal efforts of that time. Its organ, once used to accompany silent movies, was saved and moved to the state fairgrounds.

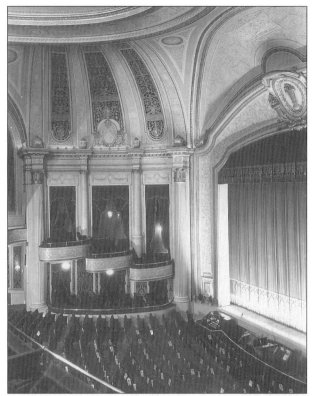

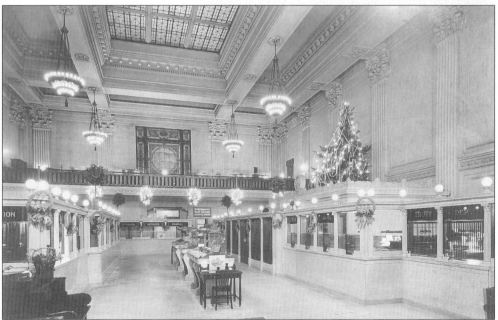

SYRACUSE TRUST COMPANY, C. 1928. This ornate neo-classical bank stood in the 300 block of South Warren Street. In addition to skylights, it featured a large stained-glass window representation of the city of Syracuse seal. It was taken over by Marine Midland and later demolished by that bank in 1962 for construction of new facilities.

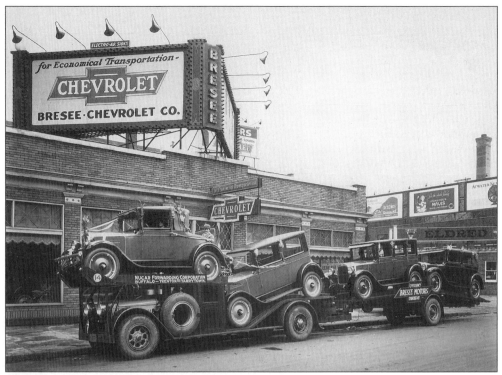

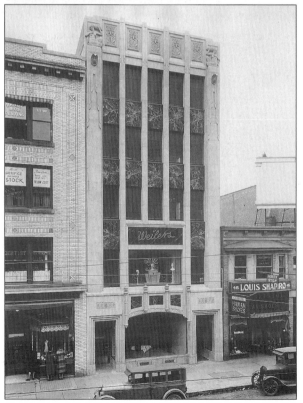

DELIVERY OF NEW AUTOS, C. 1928. Auto production soared during the Roaring Twenties as the car evolved from an indulgence for the rich into an accessible convenience for the masses. Bresee Chevrolet, one of the community's oldest auto dealers, was then located on West Willow Street with showrooms in Eastwood and downtown at South Warren and East Water Streets.

WEILER BUILDING, 1928. One of the city's best Art Deco facades of the 1920s was built in the 400 block of South Warren Street. After years of being covered during the 1970s and 1980s by an aluminum grill that hid all of its detail, it was restored in the late 1990s to exhibit again much of its distinctive style.

STATE TOWER BUILDING UNDER CONSTRUCTION, 1927. The State Tower rose as Syracuse's tallest building in the late 1920s, symbolizing the decade's optimism and reflecting the city's economic growth and prosperity. It would be the 1960s, after the Depression, World War II, and the start of office flight to James Street and the suburbs, before downtown would again see commercial construction reaching this height.

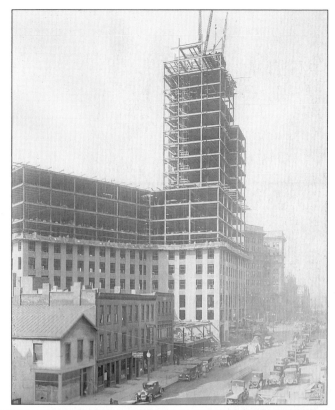

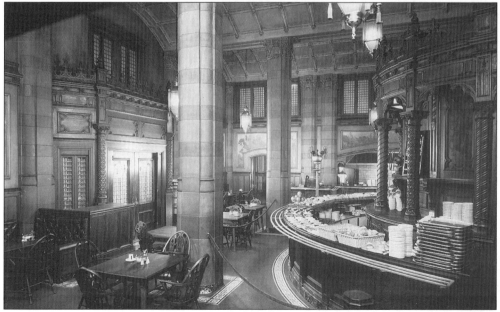

TUDOR LOUNGE, HOTEL ONONDAGA, 1926. What had been intended to function as a distinctive bar in this elegant downtown hotel had to pass the decade as a cafeteria counter during the Prohibition years of the 1920s. The noble experiment to end liquor consumption in America was a dismal failure, and Prohibition was repealed by 1933.

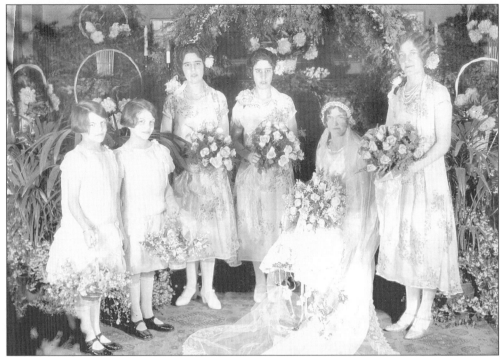

SYRACUSE WEDDING, 1925. When Margaret Miller (seated) was married to Irving Ingalls, it caused some local notoriety because three sets of twins were in the wedding party. The bride's twin was her matron of honor (right). Her two flower girls (left) were twin sisters of the groom, and her bridesmaids (center) were also twins. The loose, less restricted style of women's fashions in the 1920s are visible here.

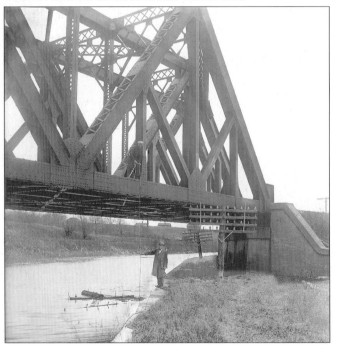

MEASURING HEIGHT OF RAILROAD BRIDGE OVER OSWEGO CANAL, 1929. Turning the stretch of the old Oswego canal running toward Liverpool into a landscaped parkway was a goal of local leaders in the late 1920s. An existing railroad bridge had been high enough for canal barges. Planners also believed it would be adequate for motorists enjoying the new Onondaga Lake Parkway. Tractor trailer truck drivers in the late 20th century would find out otherwise.

Three
1930–1947

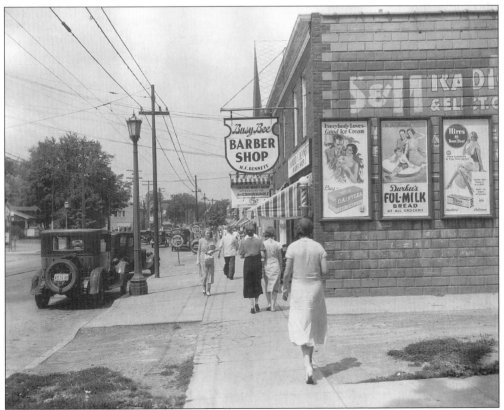

SHOPPERS ALONG JAMES STREET IN EASTWOOD, C. 1933. Syracuse's boundaries were extended to include the Eastwood area of Dewitt in 1926. Through the 1920s, city limits had steadily expanded as people sought city services and identity. James Street's path through Eastwood has continued as a viable commercial district to the present.

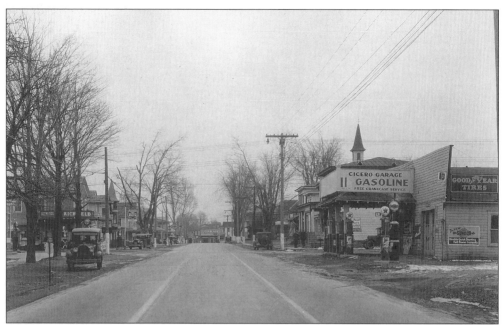

ROUTE 11 IN CICERO, 1932. The impact of the automobile's arrival on Onondaga County's rural countryside is evident in this view.

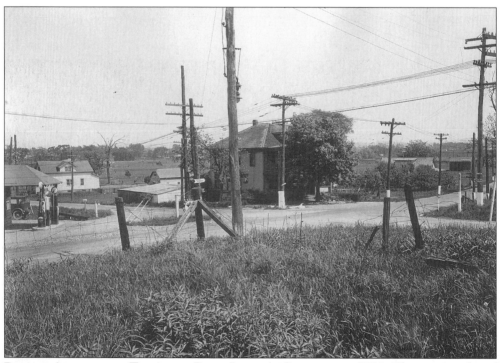

BURNET AVENUE AND THOMPSON ROAD LOOKING SOUTHEAST, 1930. The eastern edge of the city was primarily an undeveloped landscape in the years before World War II. The 1950s brought rapid suburban expansion in this direction, and this simple crossroads transformed into a busy commercial intersection.

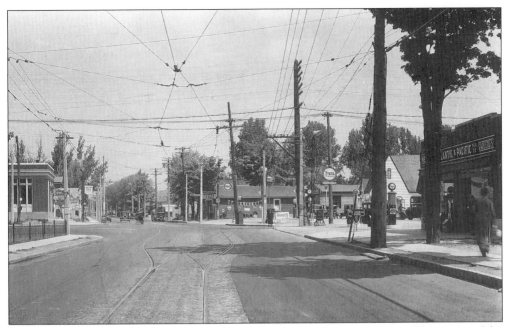

LOOKING NORTH ON SALINA STREET ACROSS SENECA TURNPIKE, C. 1930. This is one of the county's oldest intersections. In the 20th century, it has served as a commercial district for the city's Valley neighborhood.

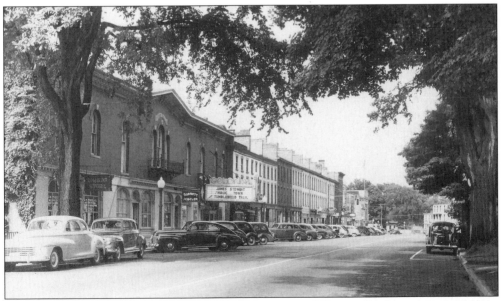

SKANEATELES VILLAGE, C. 1947. The business section of Skaneateles has retained its 19th-century character throughout the entire 20th century, no easy feat given the propensity of American society to believe newer is better. Skaneateles now can boast of a distinctive historic ambiance that most places in Onondaga County would find hard to match.

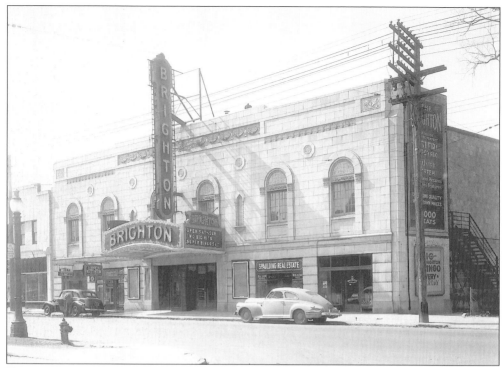

THE BRIGHTON MOVIE THEATER. C. 1945. The Brighton is an example of the many neighborhood movie houses that dotted Syracuse streets in the 1920s, 1930s, and 1940s. Downtown's movie palaces may have been bigger and more opulent, but Saturday matinees at the neighborhood cinema were a treat for an entire generation of children. The Brighton is now part of the Dunk & Bright furniture store.

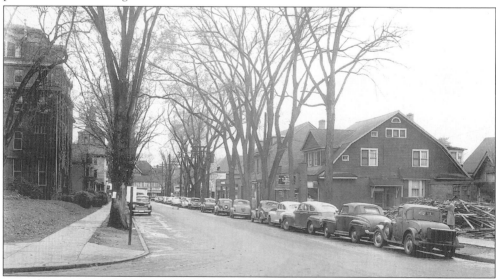

MARSHALL STREET AT UNIVERSITY AVENUE, LOOKING WEST, 1947. Although these former residences were already changing for retail use to service the Syracuse University neighborhood, the street had not yet become the boisterous commercial strip that it is known as today.

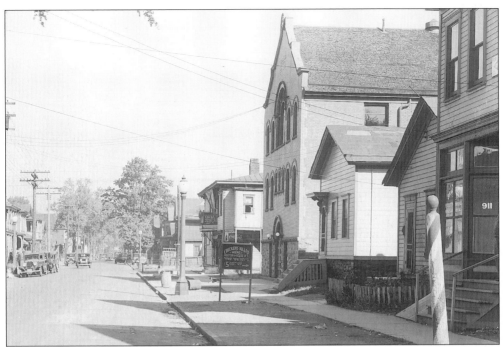

LOOKING NORTH ON SOUTH MCBRIDE STREET TOWARD ADAMS STREET, 1935. This is inside the old Fifteenth Ward, which was, for a long time, home to Syracuse's Jewish and African-American communities. The large structure (right) is the synagogue of the Congregation Ahavath Achim. This area was completely leveled to build public housing in the late 1930s.

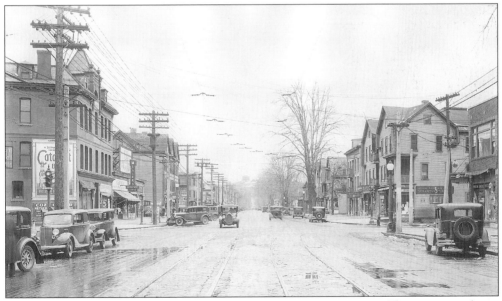

LOOKING SOUTH ON GEDDES STREET ACROSS GIFFORD STREET, 1933. This commercial area served the west end and the thousands of workers who walked and commuted to nearby factories like Franklin auto, Straight Line Engine, and Brown-Lipe-Chapin. The standpipe of Woodland Reservoir is visible in the distance.

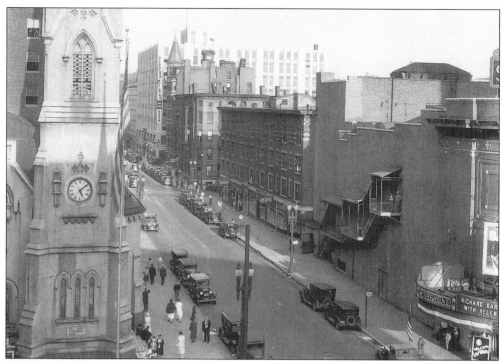

VIEW LOOKING EAST ALONG HARRISON STREET FROM SOUTH SALINA, 1931. The new Art Deco-style Syracuse Building stands out among its older 19th-century neighbors. The Strand movie theater anchors the street (right), and the steeple of the Fourth Presbyterian Church (1876) provides a dramatic counterpoint (left).

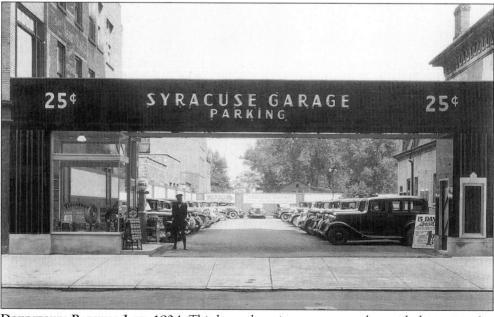

DOWNTOWN PARKING LOT, 1934. This lot and service garage, complete with distinctive Art Deco arch, stood on South Warren Street across from the entrance to the Hotel Syracuse. It is now the site of the MONY Towers complex.

44

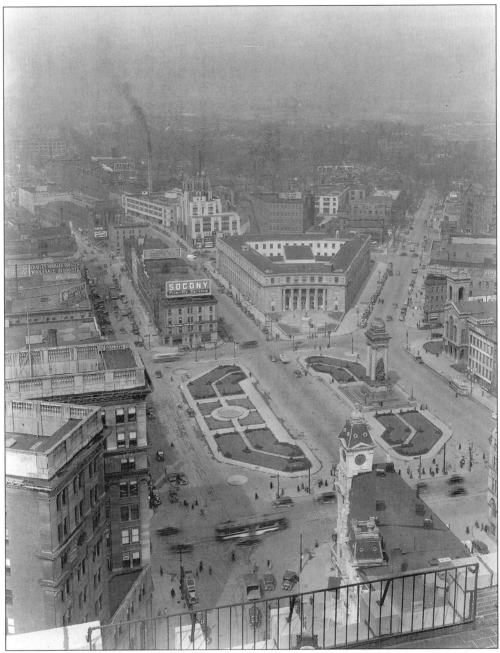

CLINTON SQUARE, 1937. The square's use as a parking lot, which followed the filling in of the Erie Canal, was replaced with this landscaping plan by 1937. Despite the hardships of surviving nearly eight years of the Great Depression, the city went about its daily life in this view from the State Tower Building.

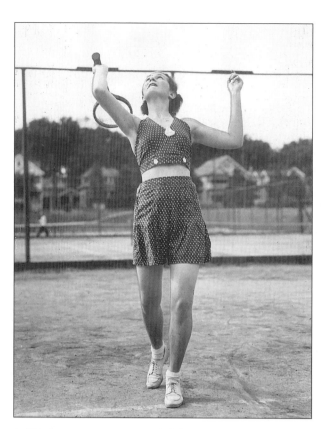

CAROLINE ANDERSON, 1936. In the 1930s, Anderson was one of Syracuse's brightest tennis stars. Her casual outfit would almost be in style today, although just 15 years before this picture was taken, its use would have been practically unthinkable.

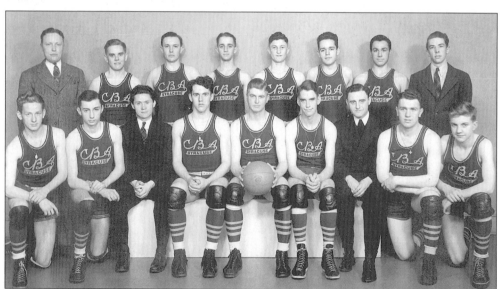

THE CHRISTIAN BROTHERS ACADEMY (CBA) BASKETBALL TEAM OF 1940-41. CBA has long had a tradition of both sports and academic excellence. When this photograph was taken, its home was near downtown on East Willow Street. Coach Pat Gleason sits third from the left. How many of these young men would face the harsh reality of World War II, just a few months into their future?

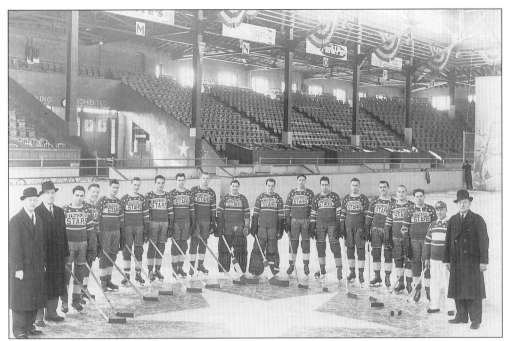

SYRACUSE STARS HOCKEY TEAM AT THE STATE FAIR COLISEUM, 1936. The 1930s meant money worries for many Central New Yorkers, but they could be proud of their local professional hockey team. The Stars were organized in 1930 and captured the American Hockey League's first Calder Cup Championship in 1937. The Depression proved a financial struggle for the Stars, and they folded in 1940.

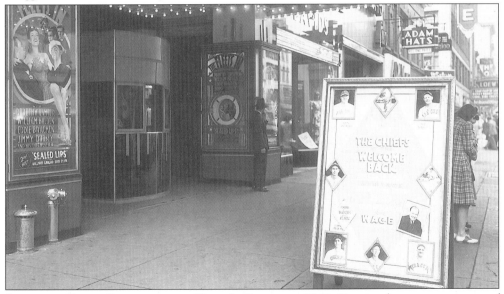

SYRACUSE CHIEFS PROMOTION AT KEITH'S THEATER, 1942. Despite the recent presence of World War II, or maybe because sports helped provide a needed escape, the local WAGE radio station hosted this "Welcome Back Baseball Party" for the Chiefs, to kick off the 1942 season. The team finished third, but behind a great pitching staff, they captured the championship Governors' Cup that summer.

47

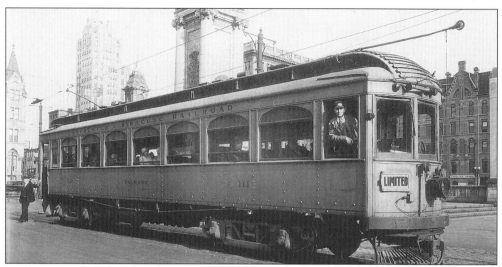

INTERURBAN CAR AT CLINTON SQUARE TERMINAL, 1931. The electric-powered interurbans provided clean, efficient transportation from cities like Syracuse to outlying communities in both Onondaga and surrounding counties. The Rochester, Syracuse & Eastern ran west from Syracuse all the way to Rochester. This line ceased operation in 1931.

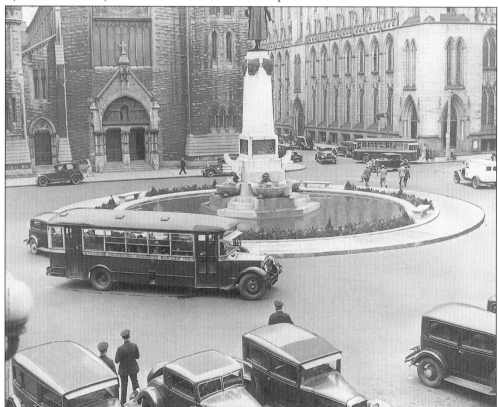

COLUMBUS CIRCLE, 1935. The latest in public transportation is seen here with two different style buses driving past the circle. By January of 1941, all municipal trolleys ceased operation in Syracuse and were replaced by the more flexible motor coach.

48

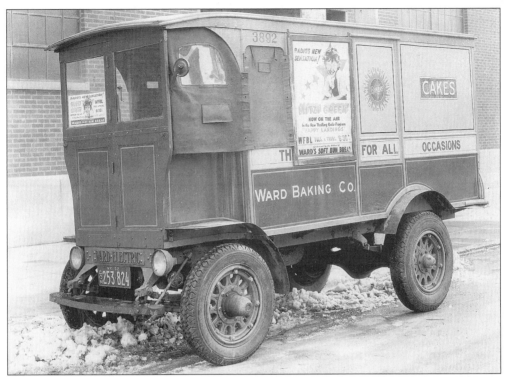

ELECTRIC POWERED DELIVERY TRUCK, 1932. Electric vehicles were rare in the 1930s, as today. The Ward Bakery was located on Shonnard Street on the city's west side.

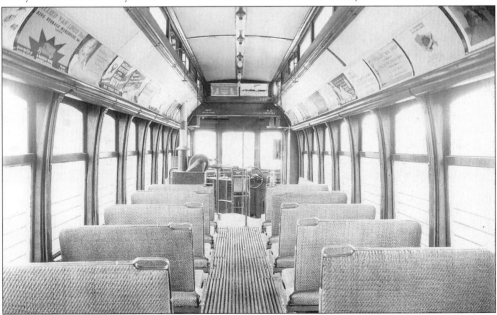

ELECTRIC TROLLEY CAR INTERIOR, C. 1934. Here is a passenger's eye view of public transit during the last decade that Syracuse used electric rail lines. This is a "double end" car that could be driven from either end. Seat backs could be flipped to face whichever way was desired. Note the stove with attached ventilation pipe to warm the interior in winter.

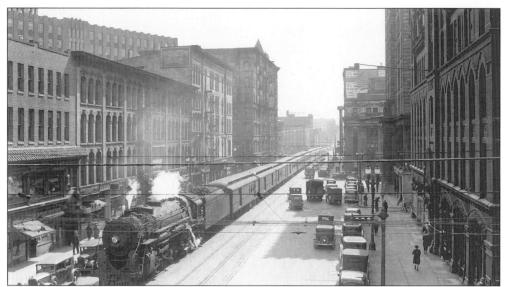

WASHINGTON STREET LOOKING EAST FROM SALINA STREET, 1935. For nearly 100 years and well into the 20th century, Syracuse had the unique distinction of sporting the New York Central Railroad's main passenger line right down the middle of Washington Street. This had become an intolerable and dangerous nuisance by 1920 and seeking a solution to the complex problem became a major civic challenge.

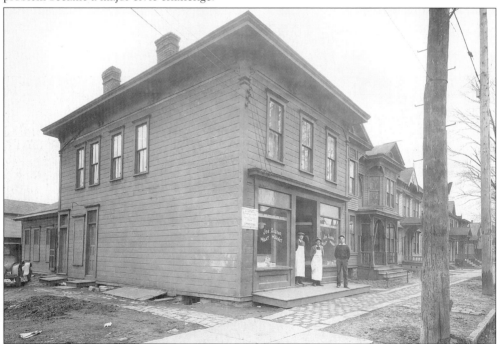

448 BURNET AVENUE NEAR HOWARD STREET, 1930. Amid great controversy, the plan to rid Syracuse Streets of numerous grade-level railroad crossings meant constructing a massive elevated right-of-way for trains through downtown. Many structures had to be removed along the south side of Burnet Avenue to build the new station, including this neighborhood meat market operated by Angelo Albino.

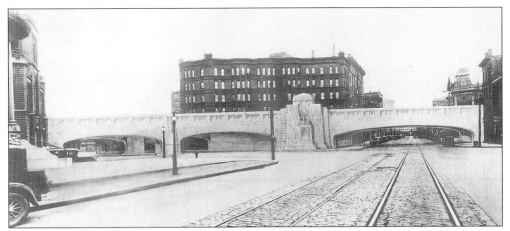

PROPOSED RAILROAD ELEVATION ACROSS JAMES STREET AT STATE STREET, C. 1930. This architect's rendering of a classical bridge with Art Deco overtones was superimposed over a photograph to help sell the concept of an elevated solution to Syracuse grade crossing woes. The massive relocation project was completed by 1941. Supported with public dollars, it helped provide needed employment during the Depression. The actual bridge built on this site, however, was decidedly less grand.

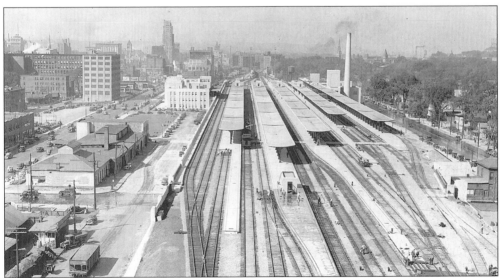

NEW, ELEVATED PASSENGER STATION FOR THE NEW YORK CENTRAL, 1936. This state-of-the-art facility, built as a key to the new elevated system, was used for only 26 years. The rapid decline in rail travel after World War II caused New York Central to build a smaller station in East Syracuse. This elevated right-of-way was adapted for the Route 690 expressway in the 1960s, although part of one platform (far right) still remained in 1999.

51

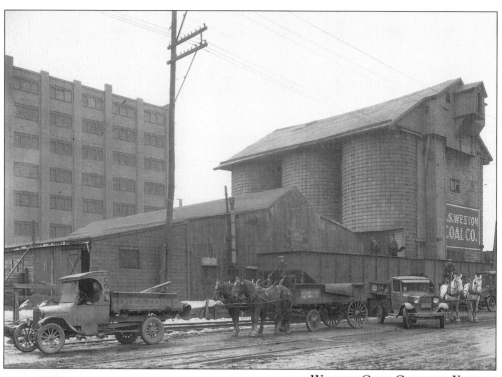

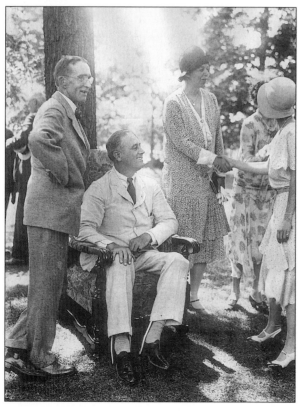

WESTON COAL COMPANY YARD ON CANAL STREET, 1930. Coal still powered the nation in the 1930s and 1940s and served as the primary heating fuel for many homes. Several coal yards, trestles, and storage sheds were nestled along railroad lines that ran through the city. Up until the late 1950s, it was a common site to see trucks delivering their dusty loads throughout Syracuse and surrounding towns.

FRANKLIN AND ELEANOR ROOSEVELT IN SYRACUSE, C. 1932. Roosevelt took a great deal of interest in the state Forestry School, adjacent to the Syracuse University campus. This view, reportedly in nearby Thornden Park, may have occurred during a visit to the school. Roosevelt's public works initiatives while governor, and later as president, were powerful tools in the effort to shake the Depression's troubles.

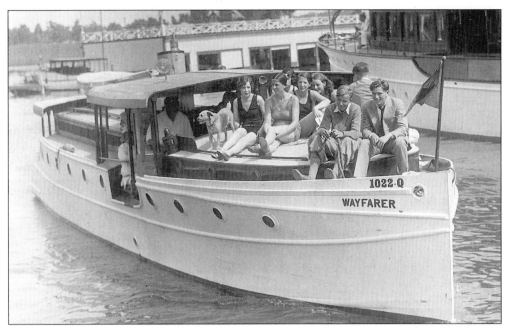

ONEIDA LAKE YACHT, 1930. This wooden inboard belonged to businessman Charles Hanna, Syracuse's mayor in the late 1920s. Here, he takes friends out to watch outboard-motor boat races on the lake. The effects of the 1929 stock market crash were not universal in bringing financial hardship immediately, nor to everyone equally.

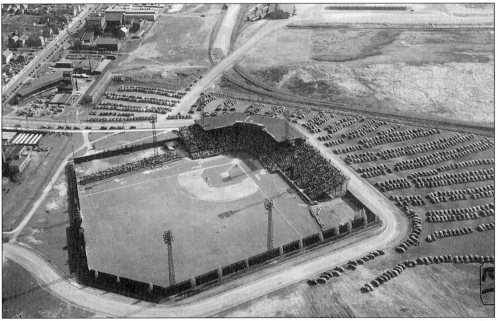

MUNICIPAL STADIUM, C. 1939. A Syracuse success in the 1930s was attracting a new professional baseball franchise back to the city. Part of the incentive was building a new stadium. Aided by public work relief dollars, Municipal Stadium opened on the north side in 1934 to host the first Syracuse Chiefs game. During the patriotic years of World War II, it was renamed after General Douglas MacArthur.

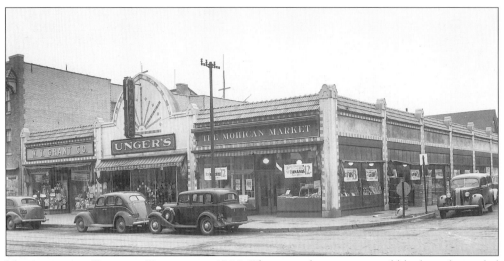

MARLBOROUGH BLOCK IN EASTWOOD, 1938. This marvelous commercial block, with its tiled roof and decorative tile trim, reflects the architectural influence of the Spanish-Colonial Revival of the 1920s. These stores are a good example of the scale of retail in Syracuse neighborhoods in the years before massive suburban growth brought large shopping plazas. In 1938, the only "superstores" were the big department stores located downtown.

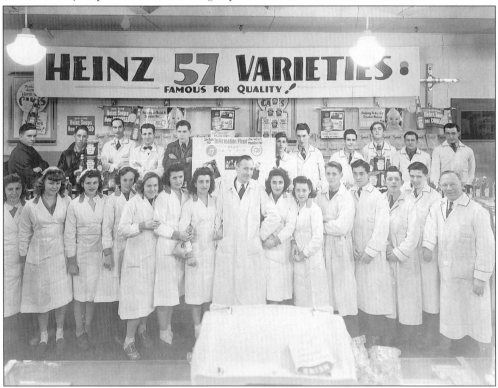

EMPLOYEES OF MOHICAN MARKET STORE AT SOUTH SALINA AND RAYNOR, C. 1944. Although there were some shortages and rationing during World War II, America avoided the destruction that enveloped much of Europe. Note the "bobby socks" and saddle shoes worn by some of the young women on the left.

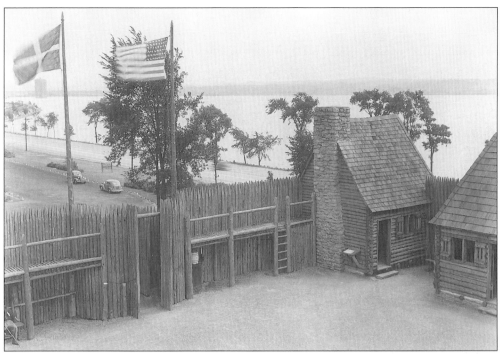

STE. MARIE DE GANNENTAHA, C. 1940. This replica of an original 1656 French settlement opened in 1933. Its construction, along with that of adjacent Onondaga Lake Park and Parkway, was carried out under early public works legislation created by then Governor Franklin Roosevelt. Known for years as the "French Fort," the site adopted a more accurate living history program in 1974. It was replaced with a more authentic version in 1991.

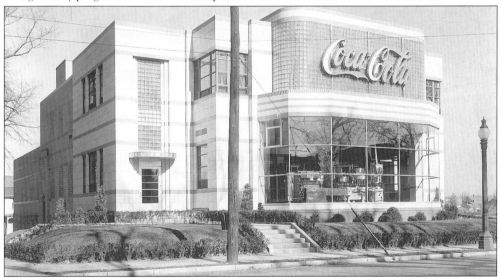

COCA-COLA BOTTLING PLANT ON WEST GENESEE STREET, 1938. With simple lines, corner windows, and use of glass block, King and King architects evoked architectural elements of the new International Style. The large windows highlighted the cleanliness and efficiency of the popular soda manufacturer's bottling operation. Later in the century, they would serve equally well for Dave Ball Chevrolet to display shiny new autos.

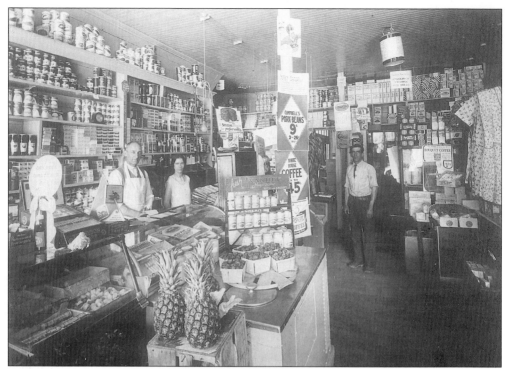

INTERIOR OF THE BITZ GENERAL STORE IN CICERO, 1930. This is a good example of the type of stores that served the several outlying village centers in Onondaga County during the 1930s. A magnifying glass shows that today's children would find the breakfast cereal section somewhat limited, with only Kellogg's Corn Flakes, Ralston Wheat Flakes, Oatmeal, All-Bran, and Quaker Puffed Rice visible.

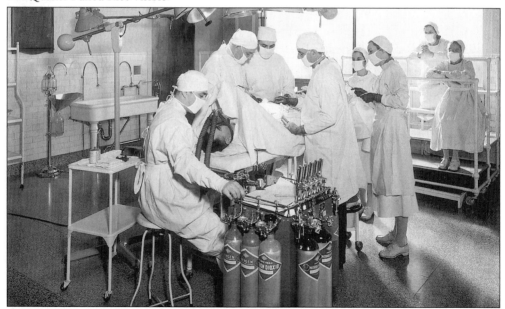

CROUSE IRVING HOSPITAL OPERATING ROOM, 1940. This was considered state of the art at the time. Note the container of ether on the rolling table (left).

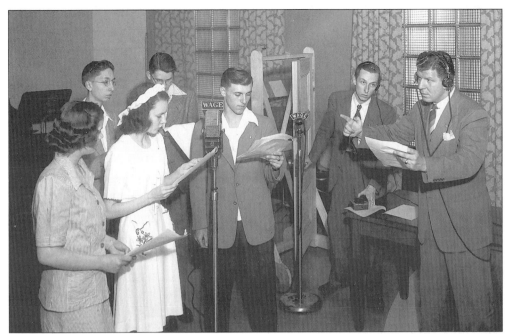

STUDIO AT WAGE RADIO, 1946. In the 1930s and 1940s, radio offered an engaging diversity of programming, including live broadcasts of dramatic plays and variety shows. WAGE was one of Syracuse's leading stations. Here, performers read their lines during a play. Note the sound-effects man ready to create the noise of a closing door.

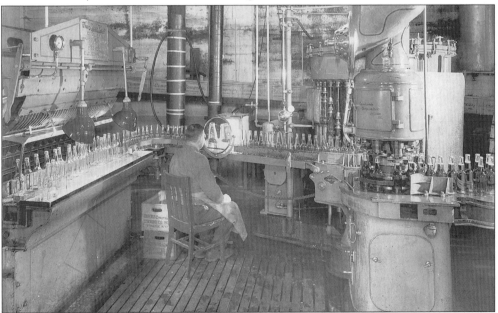

HABERLE CONGRESS BREWERY BOTTLING LINE, 1937. Syracuse developed dozens of breweries in the 19th century; however, many did not survive Prohibition in the 1920s and the Depression of the 1930s. Haberle did continue and lasted the longest, until 1962. Bottles emerge from the "Super Kleen" bottle washer (left), pass the inspector's magnifying glass, and are filled with brew (right).

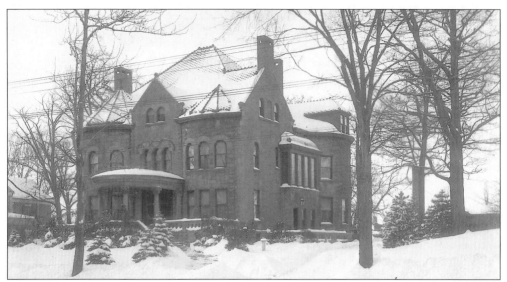

EXTERIOR OF BURNS LYMAN SMITH HOUSE AT 1045 JAMES STREET, C. 1934. The era when Syracuse's wealthy elite built ostentatious mansions on James Street had generally ended by the 1920s. The street boasted an impressive array of residential architecture up through the 1950s and 1960s. Burns Smith was of the second generation of Syracuse's great typewriter manufacturing family, and his mansion was built in the early 20th century.

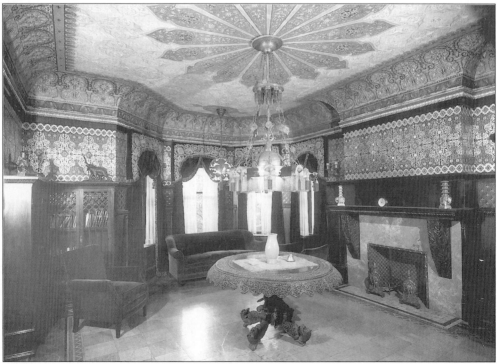

INTERIOR OF BURNS LYMAN SMITH RESIDENCE ON JAMES STREET, 1937. OHA collections include a set of photographs documenting the interior of this home. This parlor was one of the most elaborate and exotic rooms, reflecting an interest in Persian styles. This structure was later converted to offices but was demolished in 1972 for a new insurance company building.

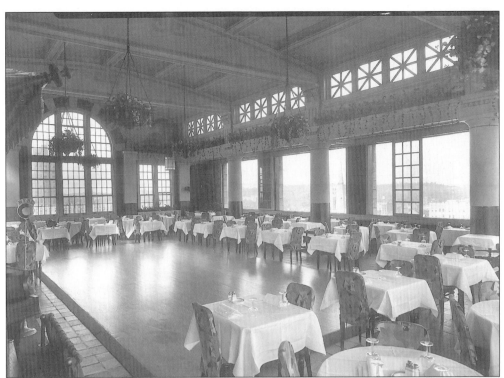

ROOF GARDEN AT THE ONONDAGA HOTEL, C. 1940. This room was one of Syracuse's most famous entertainment venues of the mid-20th century. Patrons could dance to the tunes of a live swing era band while gazing out over the lights of the city from 12 stories high. The hotel's lavish public rooms were only rivaled by its competitor, the Hotel Syracuse.

THE ONONDAGA HOTEL, C. 1934. The Onondaga opened in 1910 at the northwest corner of Warren and Jefferson Streets. It was demolished in 1970, and the site is now home to the Marine Midland/HSBC tower and parking garage. The Onondaga was an example of the classic downtown hotel found in major American cities of the early 20th century. The large windows of its famous Roof Garden are visible at the upper right.

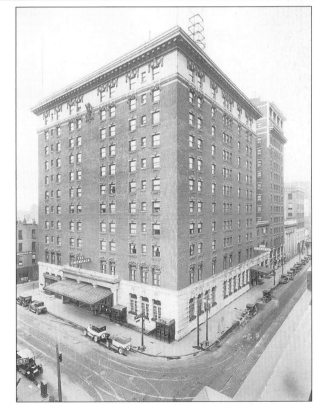

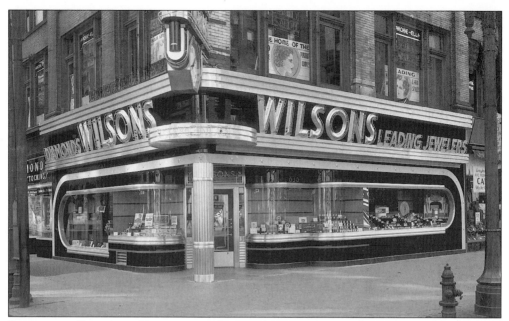

SOUTHEAST CORNER OF FAYETTE AND SALINA STREETS, 1937. The commercial building on this corner had been built early in the 20th century. By the 1930s, Wilsons, a well-known local jewelry retailer, sought a more modern and eye-catching storefront. The result was a gleaming glass, metal, and neon example of the streamline style of Art Moderne, then in fashion.

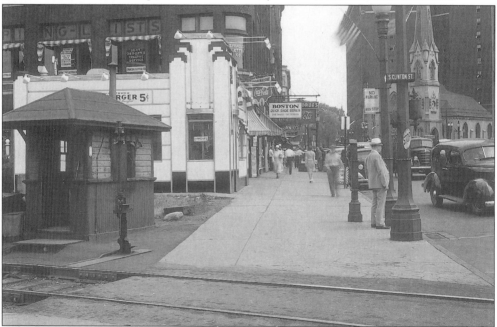

NORTHEAST CORNER OF CLINTON AND ONONDAGA STREETS, 1939. The worn railroad crossing guard shack stands in sharp contrast to the gleaming White Tower standing nearby. Along with a rival chain called White Castle, White Tower restaurants popularized the American hamburger across the nation in the 1930s. By 1999, this site had long been a parking lot. The shack and tracks disappeared when the DL&W railroad line was elevated in 1941.

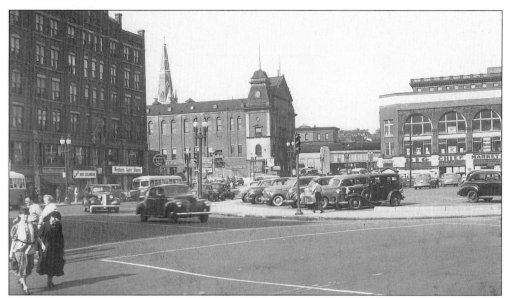

Parking Plaza at Warren Street and Erie Boulevard, 1946. Created in the 1920s, when adjacent canals were filled, this site later housed the distinctively round Kenney-Primex parking garage, from 1963 to 1981, before reverting back to an open parking lot. Note the train passing over James Street on the elevated tracks, today the path for Interstate 81.

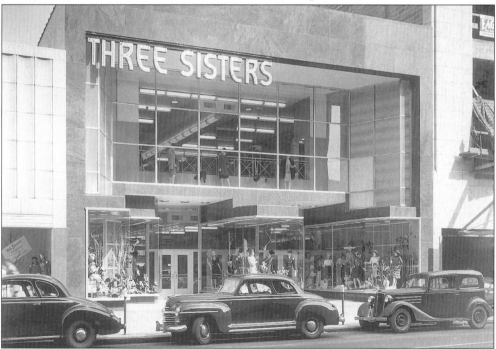

Three Sisters Store at 471 South Salina, 1946. This women's clothing store featured a very contemporary exterior for its day, reflecting the spare architectural lines that became popular after World War II. It eventually fell victim to a decline in downtown retail and was converted to the Ida Benderson senior center in 1975. It was demolished in 1980 for expansion of the Hotel Syracuse.

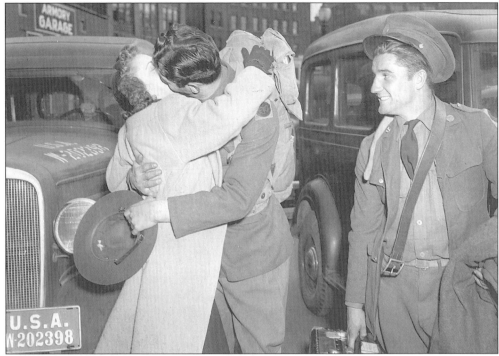

GI's AT THE JEFFERSON STREET ARMORY, C 1944. The attack on Pearl Harbor in 1941 awoke Americans from their isolationist view of the world and propelled them deep into the reality of a world war. The downtown Syracuse armory became the site of numerous emotional farewells.

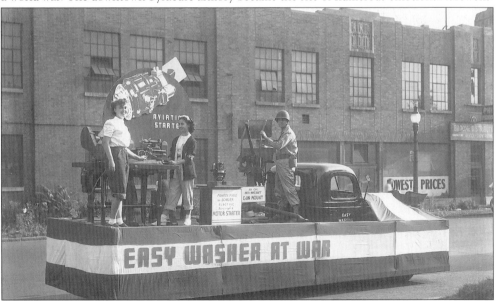

EASY WASHER COMPANY FLOAT, C. 1944. During World War II, many local industries became busier than ever making the hardware of war. This Syracuse firm switched from producing washing machines to manufacturing engine starter motors for bombers and machine gun mounts. The company asked consumers to be patient, predicting that "new-learned wartime skills will bring you the better Easy washers and ironers of tomorrow."

62

ADDIS DEPARTMENT STORE WINDOW, c. 1945. On the Central New York home front, World War II changed the style, pace, and look of life. The lack of available male workers brought many women their first and best paying jobs, but rationing limited what one could buy. Here, a downtown Syracuse department store donates its window as a recruiting tool for the Navy.

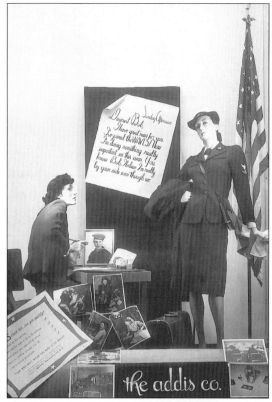

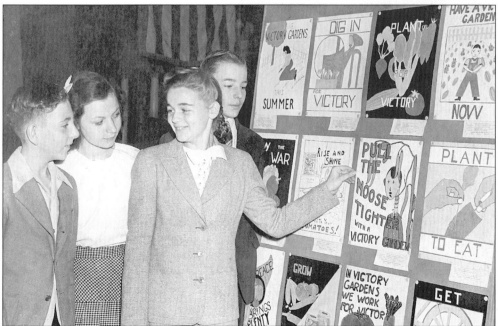

DISPLAY OF CHILDREN'S PATRIOTIC POSTERS, c. 1944. Americans were encouraged to plant backyard gardens to supplement the nation's food supply during World War II. Area school children designed posters for local promotion of these "victory gardens."

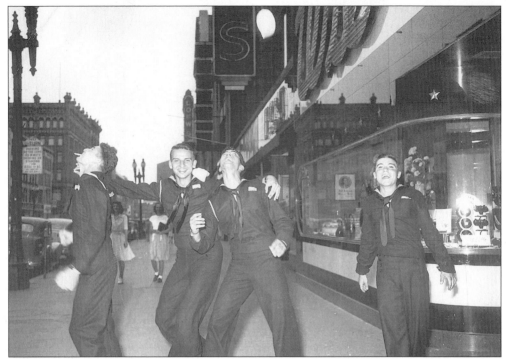

V-J Day Celebration in Downtown Syracuse, 1945. The news that the Japanese had surrendered on August 14 brought residents to the streets in a spontaneous, exuberant celebration that many believe is without equal in the 20th century. The faces of these young sailors on Salina Street say it all.

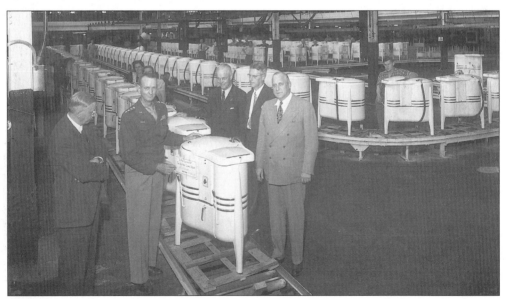

General Jonathan Wainwright at Easy Washer Plant, 1945. By October, as promised, the Easy Washer Company had returned to the production of washing machines, which were eagerly awaited by consumers. Americans' pent up savings and consumer cravings would fuel a post-war economic boom. Wainwright had relatives in nearby Skaneateles.

Four

1948–1963

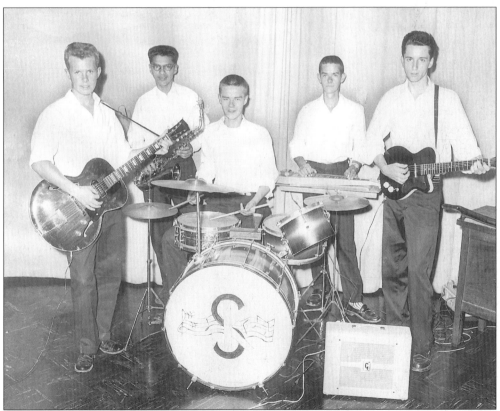

TEENAGE BAND, 1959. These five young men from Marcellus, West Genesee, and Solvay high schools organized themselves into a band called the Swingin' Keystones and played at local record hops. Elvis Presley appeared on the Ed Sullivan Show in 1956, and the rock-and-roll music he popularized helped define the post–World War II years.

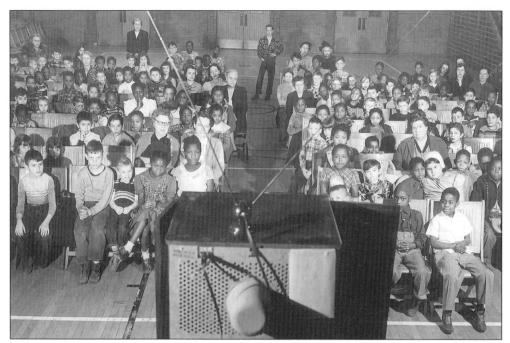

SYRACUSE SCHOOL CHILDREN WATCH PRESIDENT EISENHOWER'S INAUGURATION, 1953.
Television arrived in Syracuse in 1948 with the first broadcast by WHEN on channel 8. It would shape the baby boom generation of the 1950s and 1960s. Television's potential with children as both a creative, educational tool, as experienced here, or a source for wasted time, has been debated ever since.

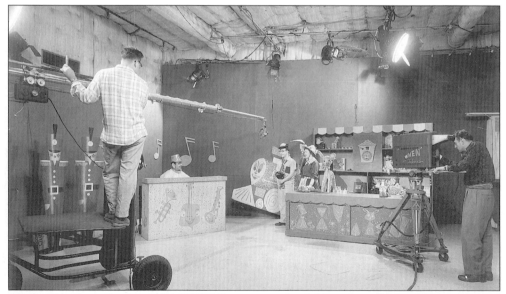

MAGIC TOY SHOP SET, C. 1956. WHEN's creation of a children-friendly, local TV program in the 1950s was a carefully researched and successful effort to use the new medium for education. The shows were scripted by Jean Daugherty (right), appearing here as the Play Lady with helper Eddie Flum Num and Twinkle, the piano-playing clown. The show ran for years and became a local, pop-culture landmark of the 1950s and 1960s.

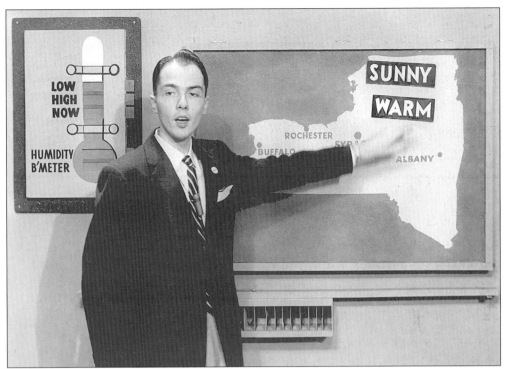

WHEN TV Weatherman Bob Oliver, c. 1955. By the mid-1950s, Syracuse had two TV stations, the original WHEN on channel 8 and WSYR on channel 3. In an era of small production budgets and before the availability of computer graphics or competition with 65 or more cable stations, the set for a local weather broadcast only needed to be very basic.

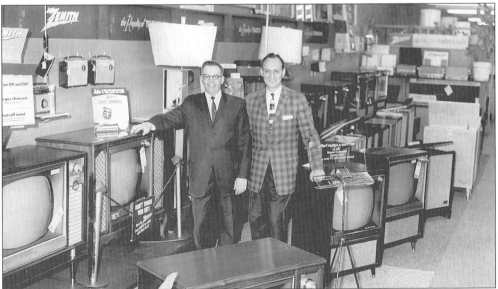

William-Morton Retail Store on Harrison Street, 1959. These furniture and appliance store owners pose in their new TV department beside the latest feature for Zenith television sets, a remote control. It was dubbed "space command," selling just one year after the U.S. had launched its first satellite into orbit.

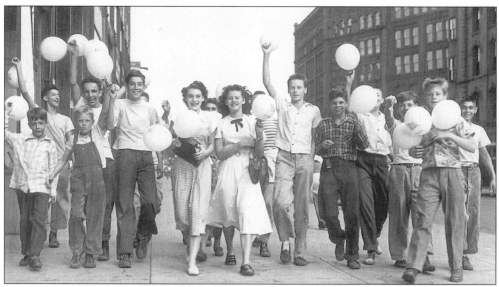

CHILDREN CELEBRATE SYRACUSE'S CENTENNIAL, 1948. The city held its 100th birthday in 1948 with an elaborate, year-long array of events and commemorative activities. With World War II past and the economy soaring, the future looked very bright. In this photograph, children walk past the State Tower Building carrying centennial balloons.

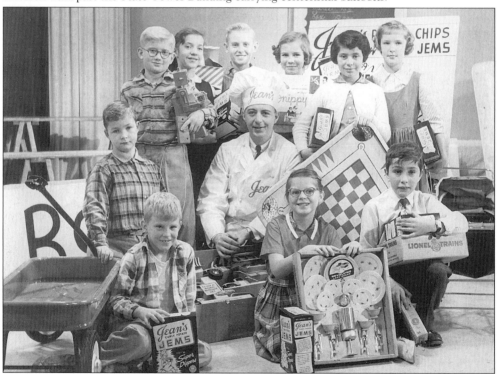

JEAN'S JUNIOR AUCTION TV SHOW, C. 1956. Host Arnie D'Angelo poses in the WHEN studios with the winners of this local children's game show. Their prizes reflect the popular toys of the day—trains, wagons, robots, and a Tonka Road Builder Set for the boys, and, of course, Snippy, an electric scissors, a doll buggy, and a pretend dinner set for the girls.

68

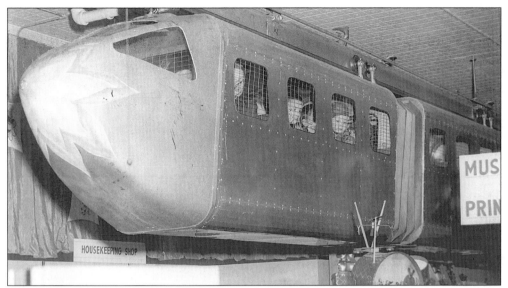

E. W. EDWARDS TOY DEPARTMENT, C. 1955. Riding the suspended monorail train in the Edwards store at Christmas is a fond memory for a generation of local children. In the 1950s and early 1960s, before the dominance of shopping malls, visiting a festively decorated downtown Syracuse at Christmas was a visual treat that many born after 1965 will never know.

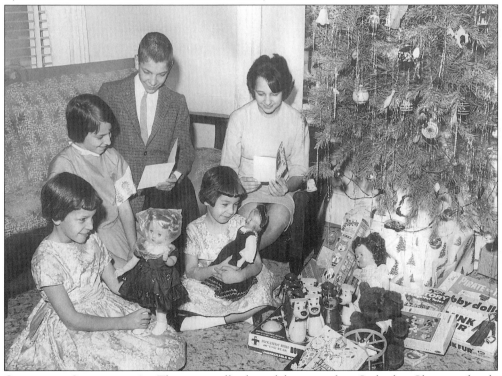

CHRISTMAS SEASON, 1962. This is actually the celebration of an Orthodox Christian family on their traditional January 7th Christmas holiday. The Metrick family had attended services at St. Peter and Paul Russian Orthodox Church on Syracuse's west side the evening before. The children could then enjoy their Huckleberry Hound bowling set, among other toys.

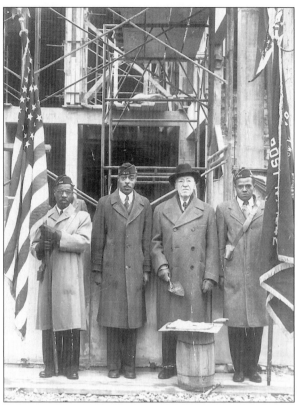

LAYING OF WAR MEMORIAL CORNERSTONE, 1950. Members of the American Legion Dunbar Post #1642 participate in this solemn ceremony, honoring 20th-century veterans during construction of the War Memorial in Syracuse.

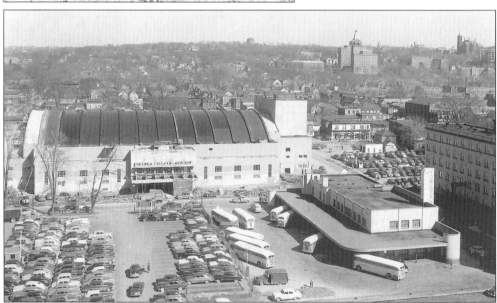

WAR MEMORIAL NEARING COMPLETION, 1951. Completion of this large civic auditorium fulfilled a community dream that had been talked about well before World War II. Also visible are the Greyhound bus terminal and, in the distance, stretching east and south toward the university, the edges of the then intact, African-American neighborhood known as the Fifteenth Ward. Harrison Street served as a commercial district of shops and services.

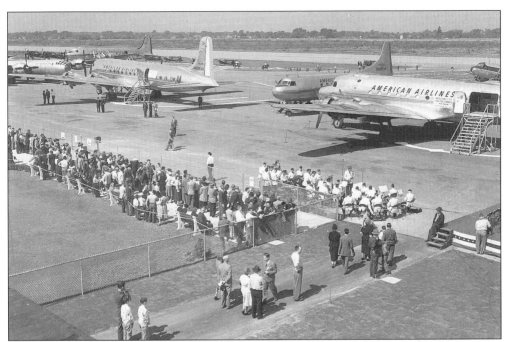

OPENING DAY AT HANCOCK AIRPORT, 1949. Hancock, a former Army Air Corps bomber training base, was taken over by the city after the war to replace its older and smaller airfield at Amboy. Thousands attended the September opening, visiting planes on display like the American Airlines Convair, C-54, and Douglass DC-6, along with the Air Force's B-29 bomber.

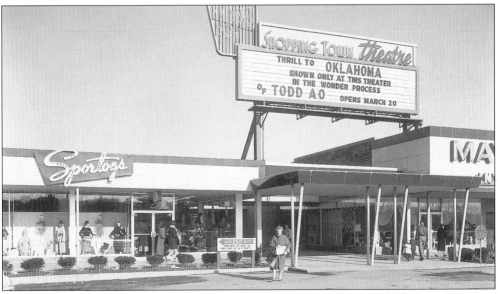

SHOPPINGTOWN PLAZA IN DEWITT, 1955. The construction of shopping plazas with acres of free parking arrived in the county by the early 1950s. One of the most ambitious was Shoppingtown, which opened in 1954. This large plaza, convenient to the expanding eastern suburbs, would eventually help signal the decline of downtown as the retail center of the community.

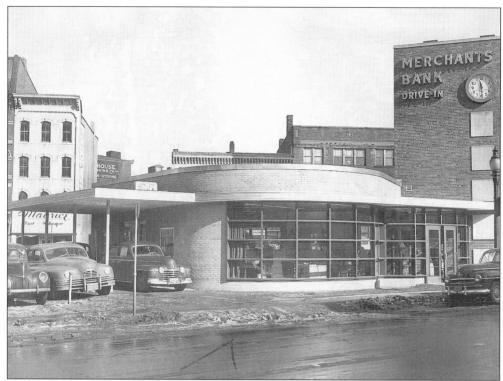

DRIVE-IN BANK AT FAYETTE AND EAST GENESEE STREETS, 1949. When Merchants Bank opened this building in 1949, it was the first banking facility specifically built for auto drive through service in Central New York and one of just a half-dozen in the state. It reflected a growing trend in the second half of the 20th century for life to be centered around the auto and the desire to save time.

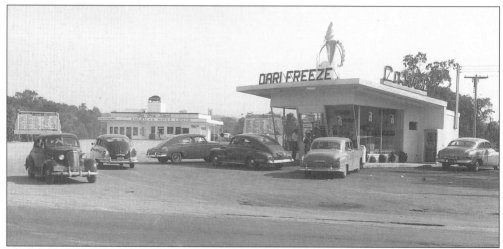

PIG STAND AND CARVEL DARI FREEZE ON EAST GENESEE STREET IN DEWITT, 1952. The Pig Stand chain started in Texas before World War II as one of America's first drive-in restaurants. Signs proclaimed, "A Meal at Your Wheel" and the billboard menu offered a "pig barbecue" sandwich for 35¢ and a ice cream cone for 20¢. In 1952, this local version had some nearby competition in the dessert department.

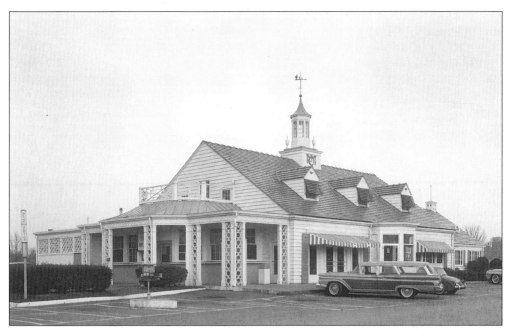

HOWARD JOHNSON'S RESTAURANT IN DEWITT, C. 1962. The distinctive colonial style of the Howard Johnson's chain made them recognizable across the country. This one on Genesee Street opened in 1941 and included waitress curb service. A sign advised customers to blink their lights for service. It was replaced with a Ground Round in 1972.

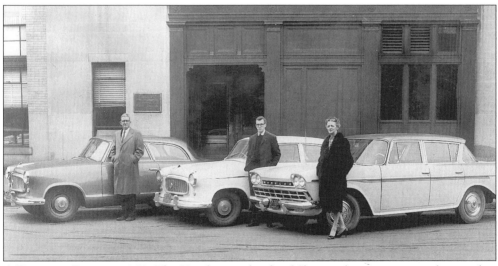

A RAMBLER FAMILY, 1960. The Hutchinson family of Skaneateles were apparently partial to Ramblers. Husband, wife, and son all bought models at Glenn Burdick Rambler in North Syracuse within a few months of each other. The Rambler line evolved from Nash and were made by American Motors until 1969.

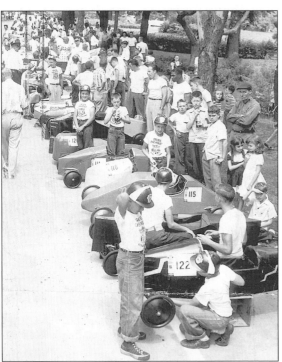

SOAP BOX DERBY, C. 1948. This one-time ritual for young boys in the mid-20th century is rare anywhere today.

CARMEN BASILIO AND FAMILY, 1955. Central New York native Carmen Basilio poses with his brothers and father after winning his national welterweight crown. He triumphed against Tony DeMarco before 9,070 roaring fans at the War Memorial Auditorium in Syracuse. It is considered a highlight of local boxing history in the 20th century.

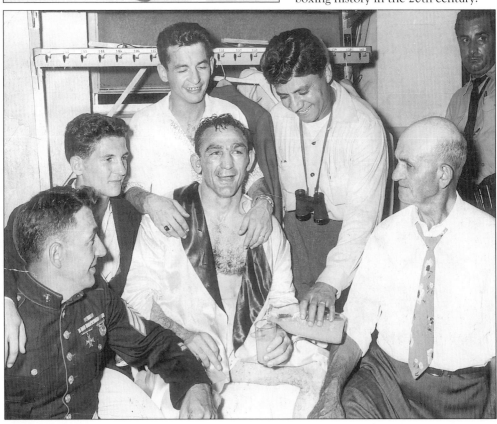

MEMBERS OF THE SYRACUSE NATIONALS PRO-BASKETBALL TEAM, C. 1955. The Nats were one of the community's most popular sports teams in the years after World War II. Coached by Al Cervi (center) and led by players (left to right) Paul Seymour, George King, Billy Kenville, and Bill Gabor, they brought the NBA championship to Syracuse in 1955.

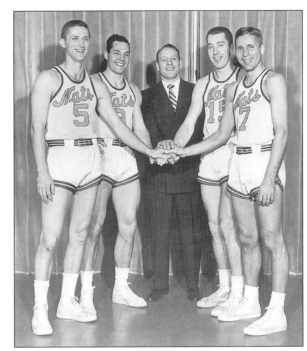

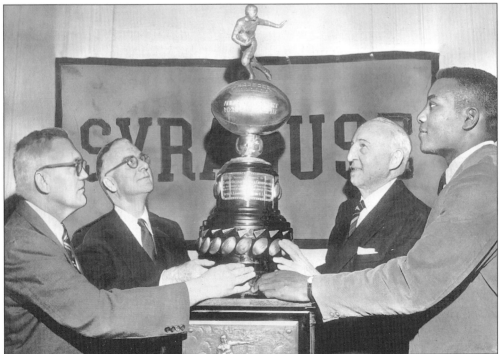

SYRACUSE UNIVERSITY FOOTBALL RECEIVES LAMBERT TROPHY, 1956. S.U. was awarded this recognition as the best collegiate football team in the East that year. Coach Ben Schwartzwalder (far left) was one reason for the team's excellence, as was their star back, Jim Brown (right). This combination later helped the team win the national championship at the 1960 Cotton Bowl.

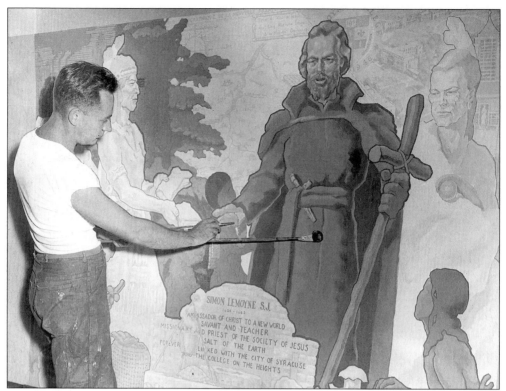

LeMoyne College Mural, 1947. The new campus of Syracuse's Jesuit-run college was dedicated in 1947. The Administration Building lobby recognized the school's namesake, 17th-century missionary to the Iroquois, Simon LeMoyne, with this painting by local artist, G. Lee Trimm.

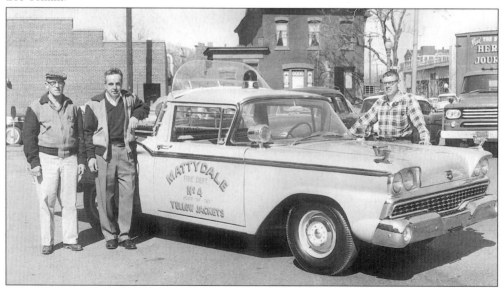

Fire Fighting Equipment, 1959. Members of the Mattydale Fire Department proudly displayed their newest vehicle, a Ford, adapted to carry firefighters and equipment to an emergency scene.

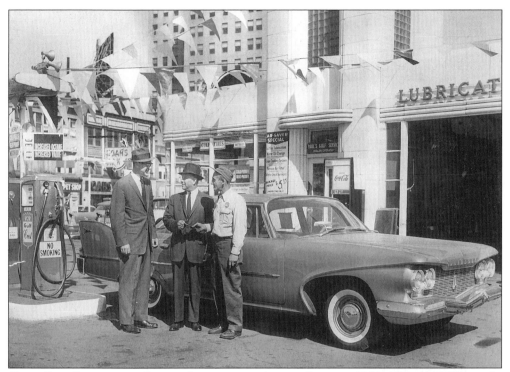

GULF GAS STATION AT SOUTH SALINA AND ADAMS STREET, 1960. This 1960 Plymouth, sporting the exaggerated tail fins popularized in the late 1950s, is parked at a classic enamel-paneled service station of the mid-20th century.

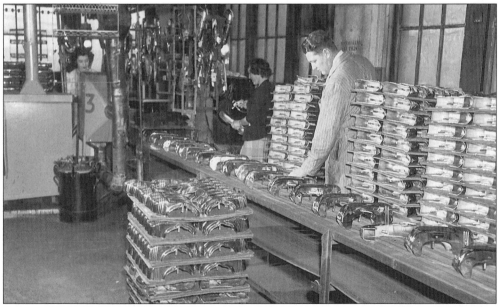

BROWN-LIPE-CHAPIN PRODUCTION LINE, C. 1950. This company produced automobile parts for General Motors from its huge plant on West Fayette near Geddes Street. It relocated to Town Line Road in Salina in 1953, functioning as a unit of General Motors. Angeline Oliva (left) sprays chrome bumper components, while foreman Jack Kurak inspects production.

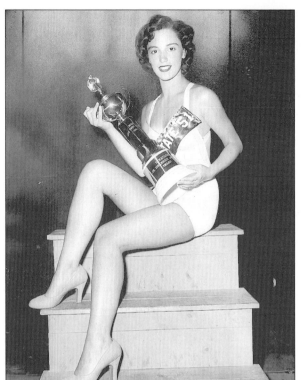

MISS SYRACUSE, 1951. S.U. freshman Louise Orlando also won the title of Miss New York State in judging at Loew's State Theater. She went on that year to compete in Atlantic City at the Miss America pageant. A local resident, she completed her music degree at Syracuse University and became a music teacher.

RONALD REAGAN AND SYRACUSE MAYOR DONALD MEAD, 1954. In the 1950s, before a political career that would lead to the White House, Reagan was a Hollywood actor, working as host of *General Electric Theater*, a TV drama series. During a promotional tour, he stopped in Central New York to visit GE's extensive Electronics Park facility in Salina.

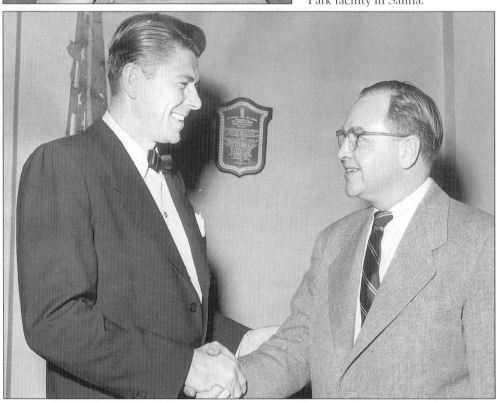

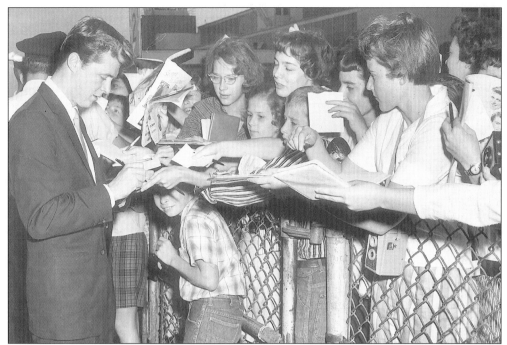

EDD "KOOKIE" BYRNES AT HANCOCK AIRPORT, C. 1959. A popular television detective series in the late 1950s and early1960s was *77 Sunset Strip*. It made a brief star of Edd Byrnes. He played the parking lot attendant, Kookie, a toned down reflection of the era's young rebel image, as epitomized more famously by Elvis Presley and James Dean.

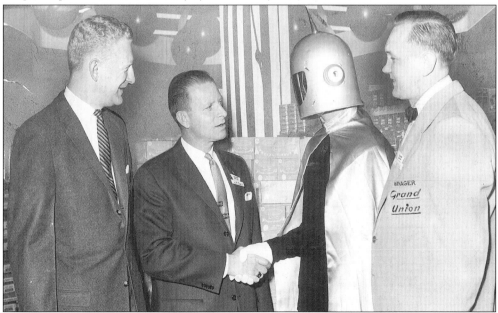

"SPACE MAN" VISITS NORTH SYRACUSE, 1959. The late 1950s saw the first successful Soviet Union and American launches of orbital satellites. Advertising agencies exploited a growing interest in space travel. This character, at a Grand Union supermarket opening, was part of a campaign for Tarryton cigarettes.

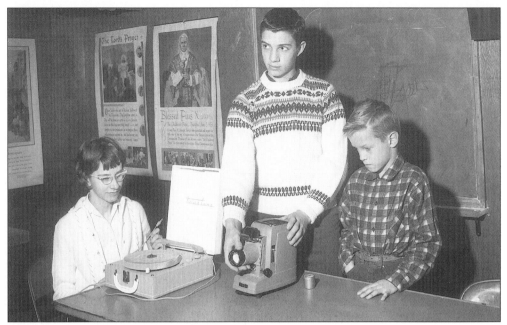

ST. JAMES CHURCH SCHOOL, C. 1960. At the end of the 20th century, most classrooms use sophisticated computers as learning tools. For students of the 1950s and 1960s, however, the filmstrip projector and accompanying record album were the standard in classroom technology.

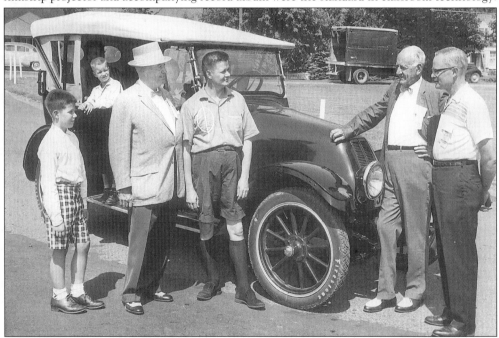

FRANKLIN TREK, 1961. Bill Cranker (center) of Toledo, Ohio, poses with his 1919 Syracuse-made Franklin Model 9B at the eighth annual meeting of Franklin owners, held at Willow Bay. His sons are at left, and the two older men on either side are former Franklin salesmen. The Franklin Car Club meets annually in Central New York. The man on the far right is R.T. Eckert, president of the Franklin Club.

CAMPUS FASHIONS, 1961. This posed photograph on the S.U. campus was included in a national *Glamour* magazine article that year.

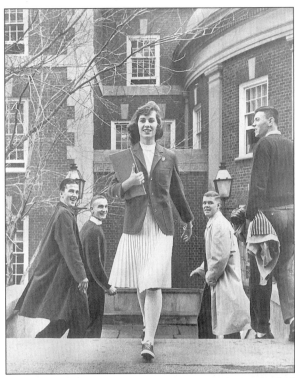

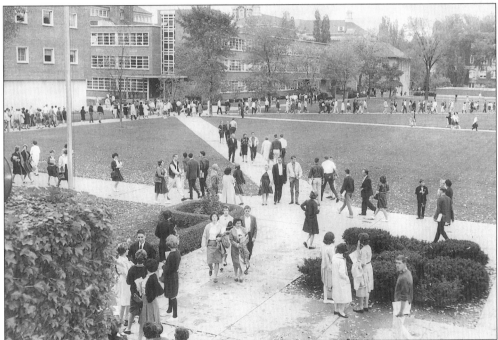

SYRACUSE UNIVERSITY QUAD, 1962. This October view proves that the above picture accurately reflects collegiate clothing styles at the beginning of the 1960s. This was a time before the Beatles had arrived from England and before civil rights and the Vietnam War had become concerns of the average student.

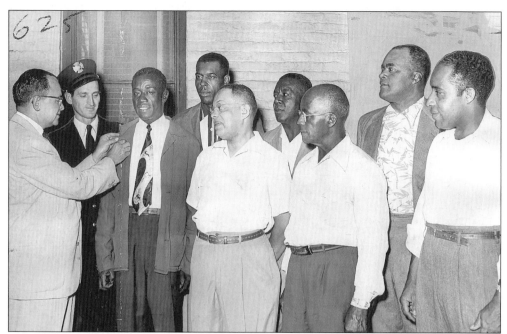

CITY BUILDING INSPECTORS, 1954. Syracuse Mayor Mead pins badges on a group of volunteer building inspectors.

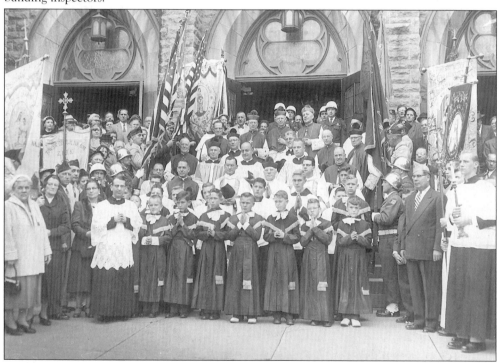

SACRED HEART CHURCH, 1955. Local Roman Catholic officials and congregation members pose on the steps of the church that serves Syracuse's Polish community. The occasion was a visit from archbishop Joseph Gawlina, a representative of the then communist-imprisoned Primate of Poland, Stefan Cardinal Wyszynski.

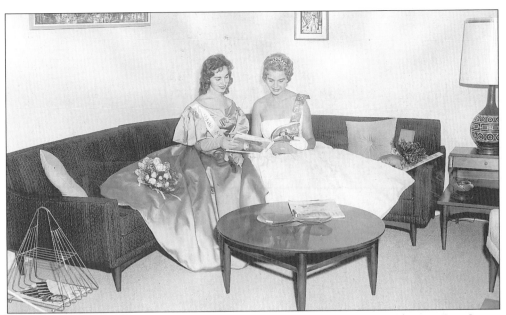

SYRACUSE "ROYALTY," 1959. Miss Syracuse Da-Laine Barfield (left) and State Fair Queen Carol Youman pose in a model home. The furniture is a good example of the spare, angular, "modern" lines popular in the 1950s and early 1960s.

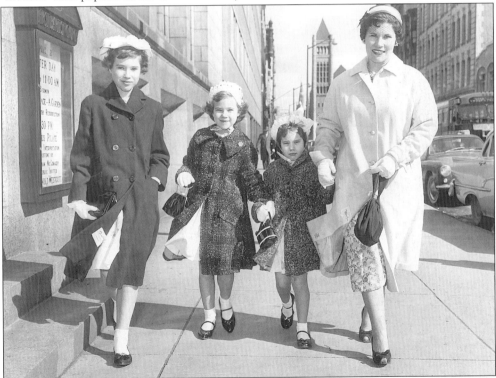

EASTER SUNDAY, 1961. The Teachout family of North Syracuse shows what was proper Sunday church attire in the early 1960s. They are walking south on Montgomery Street in downtown, past First Baptist Church.

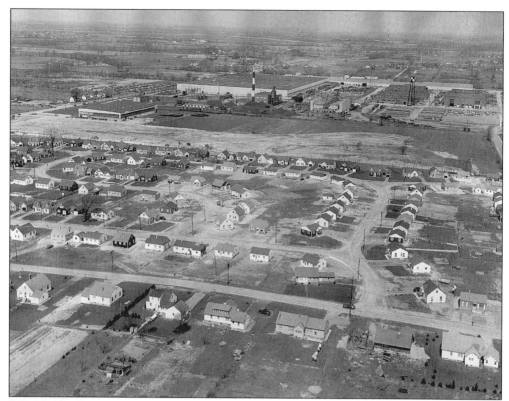

PARKWOOD DEVELOPMENT EAST OF THOMPSON ROAD, 1952. These homes are a good example of the style of post–World War II construction that occurred around the rim of the city in order to provide much-needed housing for returning veterans and their new families. Original prices for these models were around $9,000. The Carrier plant is in the distance.

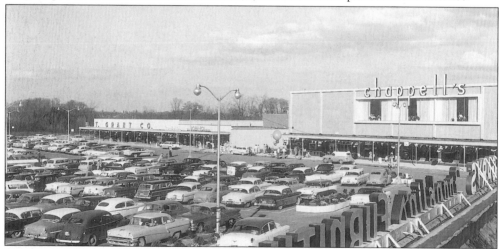

OPENING OF CHAPPELL'S NORTHERN LIGHTS STORE, 1956. In the 1950s, this venerable Syracuse department store joined the rush to suburban shopping plazas since these locations represented the future of retail. Among its new "neighbors" in Mattydale were Dixie Hats and Sam's Hobby & Toy Center. In 1999, Northern Lights remains, with the Media Play chain occupying Chappell's former building.

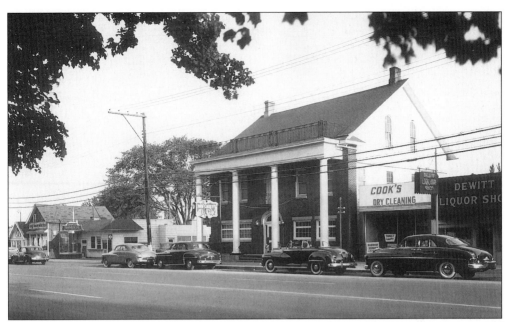

EAST GENESEE STREET IN DEWITT, 1950. This commercial stretch of Genesee, just west of Erie Boulevard, grew from its 19th-century roots as Orville, a small business center in the town of Dewitt. In the late 1920s, suburban expansion began to transform it. Ben Casey's Inn became Walter White's Restaurant in 1965. This historic building burned and was lost in 1979.

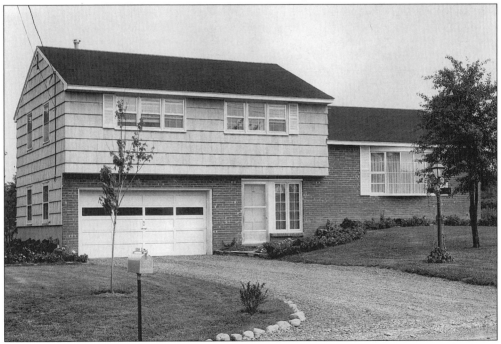

BERKSHIRE MANOR DEVELOPMENT IN MANLIUS, 1959. This was considered one of the latest looks in county housing at the time. It represented the great American dream and reality of the last half of the 20th century—leaving the city and owning your own four bedroom, 2 $^1/_2$ bath home in the suburbs.

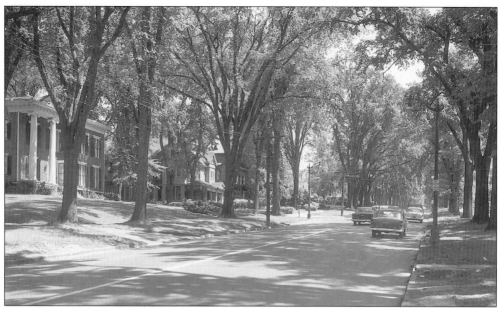

JAMES AND HIGHLAND STREET LOOKING EAST, 1957. Large mansions framed by towering elms made James Street one of the state's grand avenues of 19th and early-20th-century architecture. An unforgettable loss, the sites were being rezoned and cleared for commercial use by the 1950s, as changing lifestyles and fortunes made these urban estates obsolete as single family residences. Eventually, disease would also spell doom for the majestic elm trees.

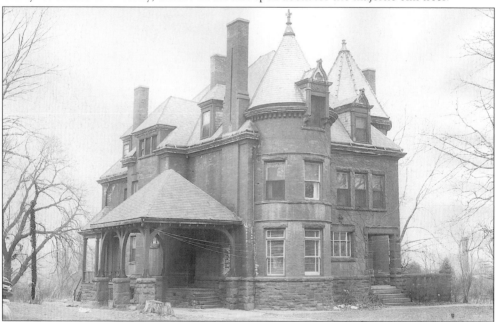

ROBERT AND MARY DEY HOUSE AT 950 JAMES STREET, 1957. Built in the late 19th century, this was the home of Syracuse's department store tycoon and his wife, a founder of Syracuse's Memorial Hospital. It was demolished shortly after being photographed. The large lot size of James Street mansions were adaptable for low rise office buildings, which could be surrounded by their own parking lots. Dozens of these landmarks were lost in the 1950s and 1960s.

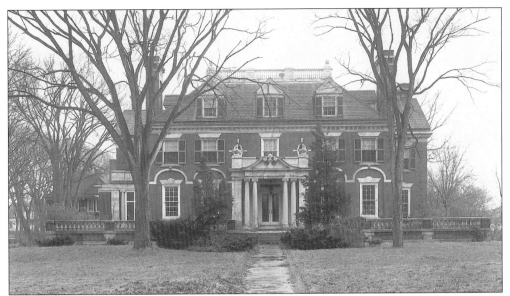

HOLDEN MANSION AT 1100 JAMES STREET, C. 1961. Built in 1902, this Georgian Revival treasure was leveled in the early 1960s to make way for a motel. The mansions of Rochester's counterpart to James Street, East Avenue, started to undergo the same demolition fate, but that city passed historic district legislation in 1968 to stop it. Many were saved and successfully renovated for new uses.

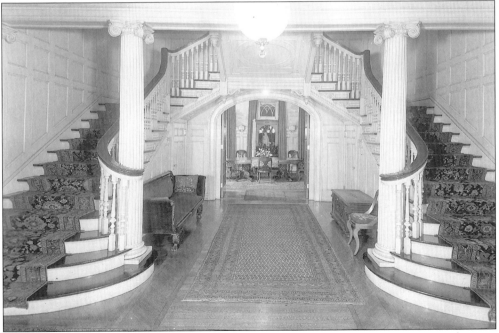

HOLDEN MANSION INTERIOR, C. 1950. This grand entry was part of the classic design executed by local architect Albert Brockway for Holden, a wealthy "capitalist" and state senator. The 1960s complex on this site today marks the eastern end of the commercial "office park" development that took all but a handful of Syracuse's most stately 19th and early-20th-century residential architecture.

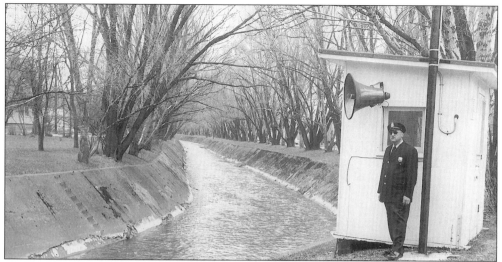

ONONDAGA CREEK WATCHTOWER, 1963. The waters of Onondaga Creek caused south side flooding problems for decades. In the early 20th century, it was channeled to help keep flow within its banks, but this made its current dangerously swift. To protect against children drowning, watchtowers with creek patrolmen were built. Eventually, fencing was installed.

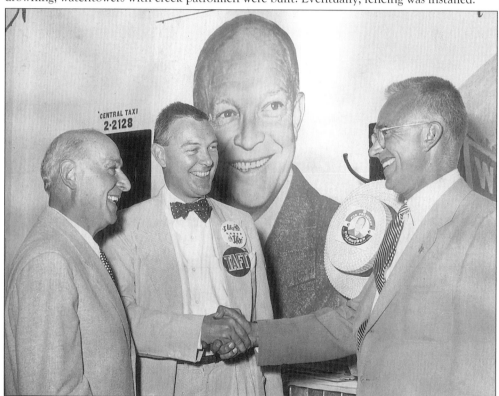

PRESIDENTIAL CAMPAIGNING IN SYRACUSE, 1952. Local Taft and Eisenhower boosters (left to right), Hiram Weisberg, Burton Kehoe, and William Morton, look forward to a Republican win. This was the first presidential election where TV played a major role in selling candidates. "Ike's" victory made him a national symbol for the prosperous decade of the 1950s.

"ATLANTIC WEATHERMAN" RON CURTIS, C. 1960. Like many early TV personalities, Curtis moved over from radio announcing. He had worked at local radio stations WFBL and WHEN before joining WHEN-TV as weatherman and announcer. He advanced to news anchor in 1966 and, in maintaining that position for the next four decades, became a Central New York media icon.

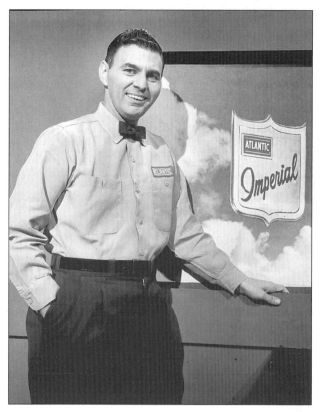

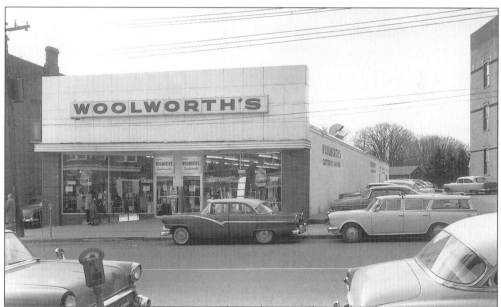

WOOLWORTH'S IN BALDWINSVILLE, 1961. This chain of nationwide five-and-dime stores began in 1879, founded by Frank Winfield Woolworth, a native of nearby Jefferson County. Store size varied, depending on the community. Several were scattered across Central New York for much of the 20th century, but the end of the 1990s left none in Onondaga County.

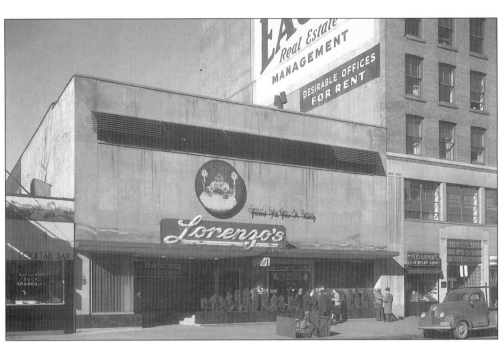

LORENZO'S RESTAURANT, 1948. Lorenzo's, on South Salina near West Onondaga Street, was one of downtown Syracuse's popular nightspots in the years following World War II. It offered an entrée into the community for one particularly ambitious young man, by providing him work as a bartender while finishing law school. Lee Alexander later rose through the political ranks to become mayor of Syracuse in 1970.

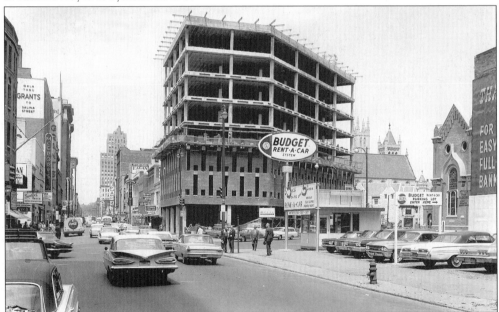

CONSTRUCTION OF 499 SOUTH WARREN AT EAST ONONDAGA STREET, 1963. Syracuse Savings Bank's new building housed a branch operation at ground level and rented office space above. It was one of many construction projects during the 1960s that reshaped a great deal of downtown, erasing much of its lingering late-19th and early-20th-century appearance.

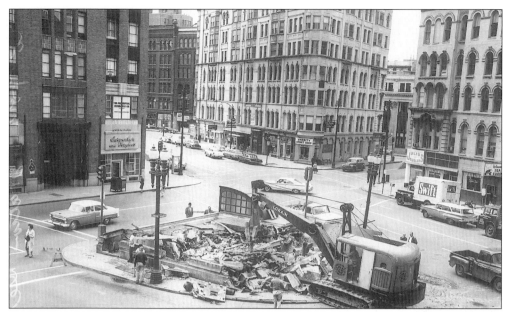

DEMOLITION OF HANOVER SQUARE'S PUBLIC REST ROOMS, 1962. A remnant from the early 20th century disappeared as city leaders sought to modernize the image of downtown. Much of Hanover Square was listed for demolition in the urban renewal plans that were developed in the 1960s. Small lot size made redevelopment difficult, and by 1976, Hanover Square survived to become Syracuse's first historic district.

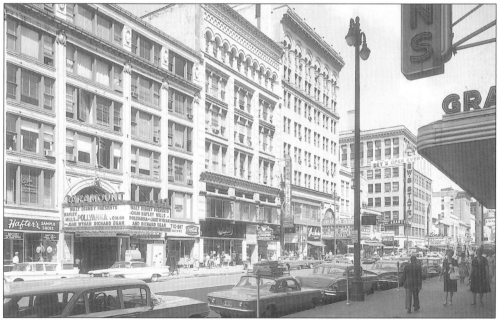

400 BLOCK OF SOUTH SALINA STREET, 1960. The 1950s was the first decade that Syracuse's population had shrunk, from a high of 220,583 to 216,038. That trend would accelerate during the rest of the century. Despite a growing number of available suburban shopping and movie alternatives as the 1960s began, downtown still remained the center for retail and entertainment variety.

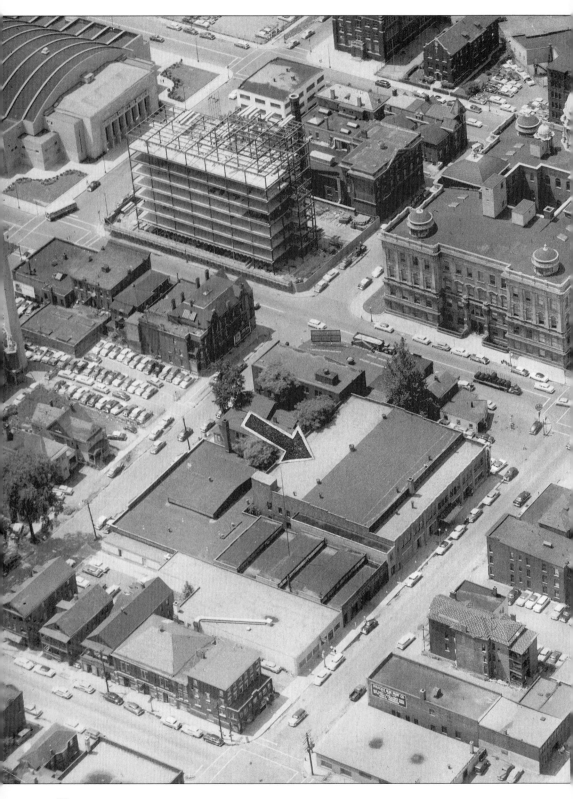

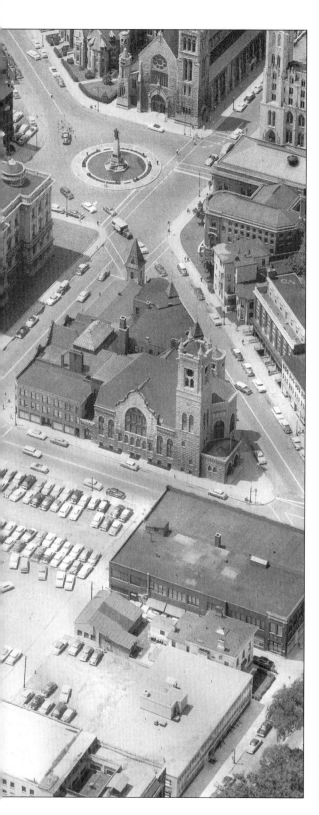

"Community Plaza" Redevelopment Area, 1957. Local leaders had been discussing the need for a new civic building complex as early as the 1920s. The Depression and World War II brought delays, but by 1951, construction of the War Memorial Auditorium (upper left) had completed one goal. In 1957, a new county office building was underway. By 1960, land was acquired east of the courthouse, including the Jefferson Bowling Academy (arrow), as plans for a "community plaza" progressed. Note the scattered presence of 19th-century residences.

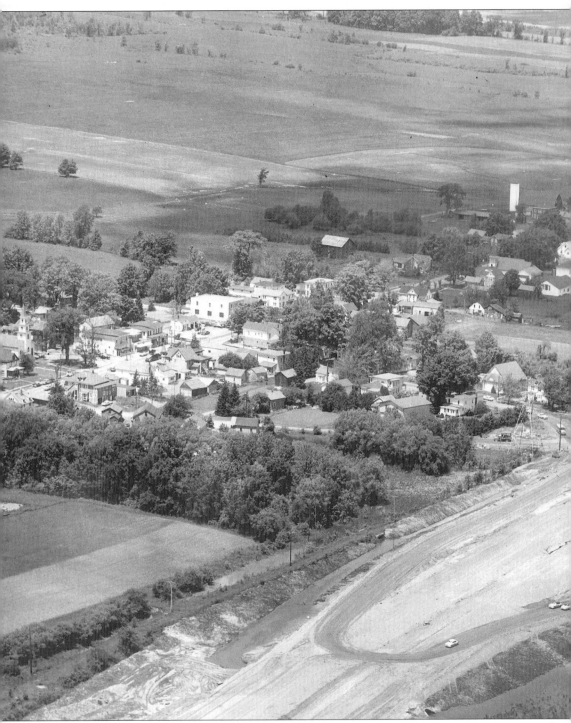

"Empire Stateway" Crosses Route 31 at Cicero, 1958. This expressway was part of constructing a cross-country, interstate highway system, undertaken as a national goal in the 1950s. This portion eventually became part of Route 81, which opened in sections between Binghamton and the Thousand Islands throughout the 1950s and 1960s. Note the compact

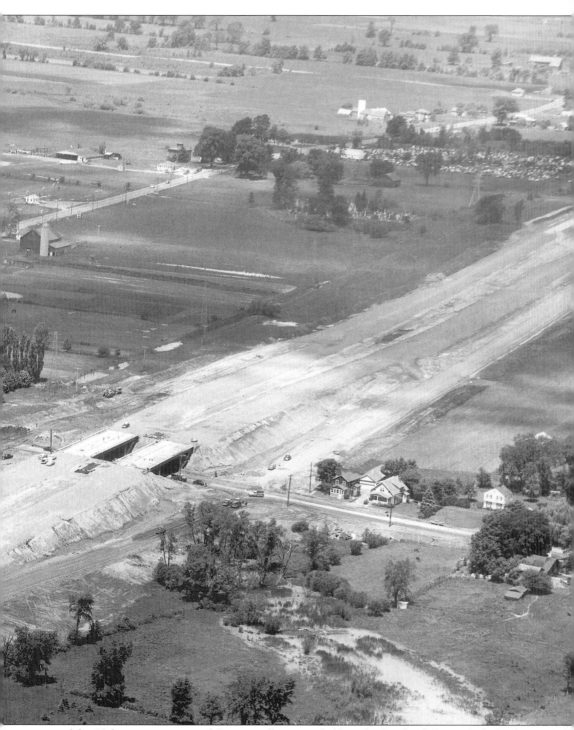

nature of the 19th-century center of Cicero, still surrounded here by farmland. Route 81 helped foster amazing suburban growth in the northern part of the county during the last quarter of the 20th century.

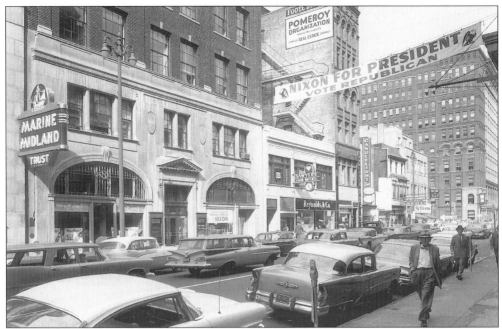

SOUTH WARREN STREET LOOKING NORTH TO FAYETTE STREET, 1960. This October view shows the hotly contested presidential election of 1960 in full swing. Most of this site was developed as offices for Blue Cross and Blue Shield of Central New York later in the century.

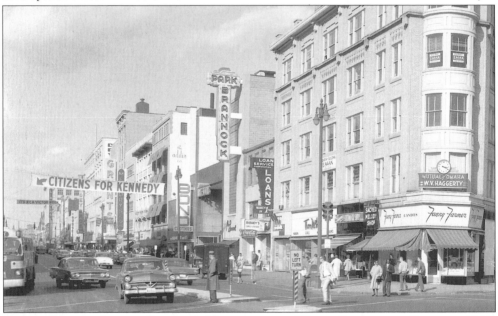

SOUTH SALINA STREET LOOKING NORTH FROM WEST ONONDAGA STREET, 1960. Democratic supporters promote a senator from Massachusetts as their presidential hope at the beginning of a decade that would witness intense upheaval, change, and conflict. None of it was envisioned by the downtown shoppers going about their business on this October afternoon. The triangular McCarthy Building would fall in 1980 to make way for an addition to the Hotel Syracuse.

Five

1964–1974

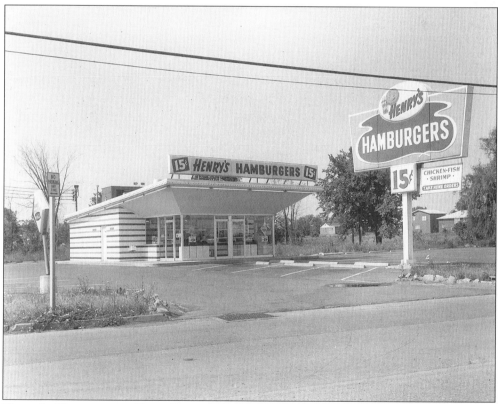

HENRY'S HAMBURGERS FAST FOOD STAND ON NEW COURT AVENUE, 1966. Although eateries catering to automobile motorists had developed in the 1920s, the 1960s saw an increase in number and variety. In upstate New York, Henry's, McDonald's, and locally developed Carrol's all featured similar, angled-roof drive-ups and 15¢ hamburgers. Carrol's evolved into Burger Kings, McDonald's became worldwide, and Henry's is just a memory.

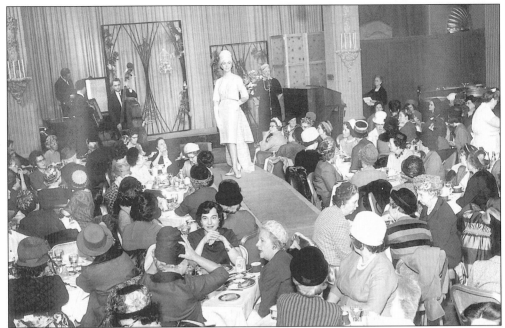

FASHIONS AT LUNCHEON, 1964. This was a long-running WHEN-TV production broadcast from the Persian Terrace of the Hotel Syracuse. Going downtown to lunch in the mid-1960s still meant wearing a fashionable hat for most women.

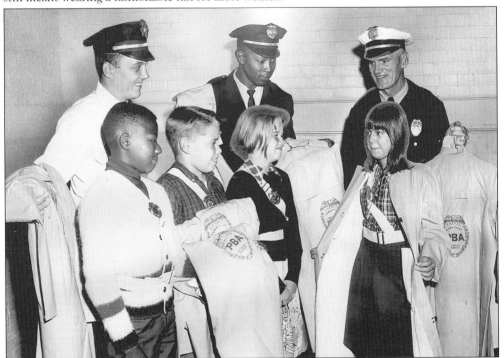

DANFORTH SCHOOL SAFETY PATROL, 1965. Policemen Earl Hennessy, Herman Edge, and John Galvin distribute new rain coats to patrol members. In the 1960s, wearing these white canvas belts and shiny patrol badges was a special honor for those selected.

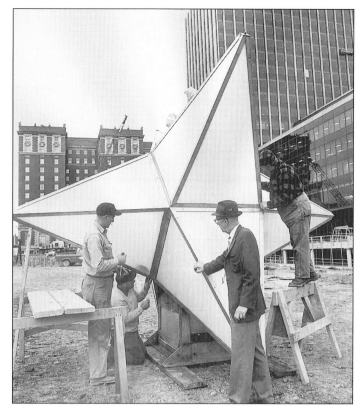

MONY WEATHER STAR, 1966. The construction of the Mutual of New York office tower was a major symbol of downtown urban renewal efforts of the 1960s. The famous weather star, rising high above its roof, has been a distinctive local landmark for the last four decades of the 20th century.

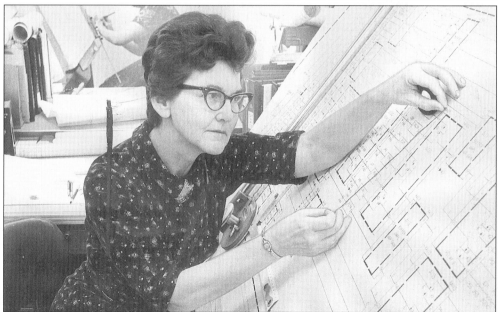

GE "DRAFTSMAN" AT ELECTRONICS PARK, 1965. Pauline Rowe won a company award from General Electric for her suggestion that black tape be used on electronic circuit drawings instead of drawing lines by hand. With today's personal computers, drafting tape has almost become as antiquated as the slide rule.

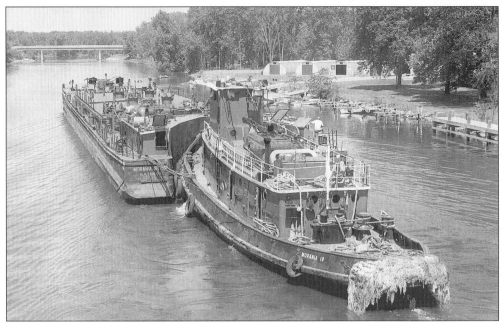

Tugboat and Tanker Barge enter Onondaga Lake Outlet, 1973. Onondaga Lake's southern shore developed after 1920 as a yard for regional oil storage. Oil was shipped in by canal barge and piped to holding tanks, creating the district known as "Oil City." By the 1990s, most oil was transported by underground pipelines, allowing relocation of the tanks and the ongoing redevelopment of the lake front as an entertainment and shopping sector.

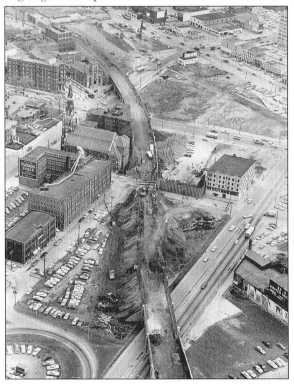

Route 81 Under Construction in Downtown Syracuse, 1966. The construction of a North-South interstate through New York continued into the mid-1960s, with the route cutting through the middle of downtown. This view shows conversion of the former New York Central elevated rail line of 1936 into the highway. St. John the Evangelist Church is at the center of this photograph, with the old St. Peter's Church visible above it.

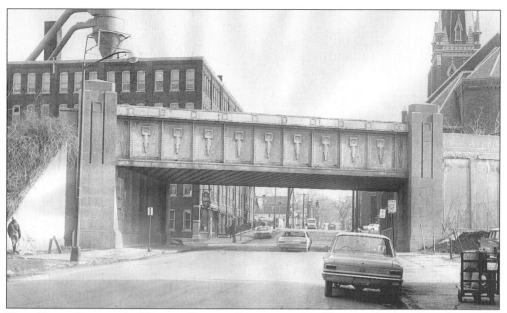

NEW YORK CENTRAL'S WILLOW STREET BRIDGE, 1966. This simple Art Deco design was installed when Syracuse elevated its train tracks in 1936. It only lasted 30 years. The tracks were abandoned when passenger train traffic dropped throughout the 1950s. This viaduct was replaced with a plain concrete highway bridge for the Route 81 interstate.

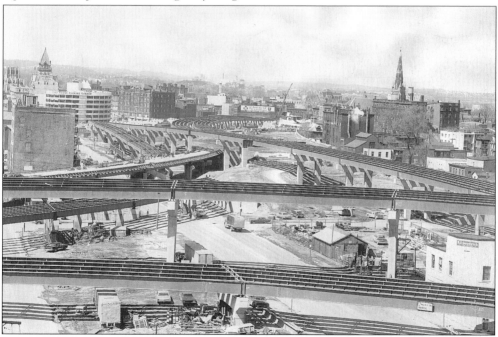

ROUTE 81 AND ROUTE 690 INTERCHANGE, 1967. This view shows just some of the massive amount of clearance required by the construction of these two highways, in an area dubbed the "can of worms" by construction workers. Route 81's path removed much of the neighborhood that once stood southeast of downtown and essentially erected a wall between the latter and the growing University Hill section.

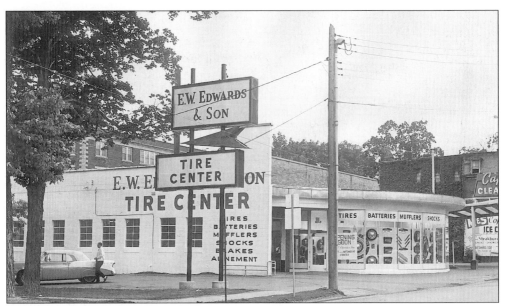

E.W. Edwards & Son Tire Center at 1543 South Salina Street, 1964. This marked an effort by one of Syracuse's traditional downtown department stores to capture more of the growing auto service business. They especially hoped this "convenience" store would attract more women who, by the mid-1960s, were handling an increasing amount of responsibility for family car repairs.

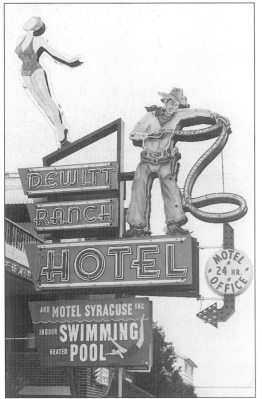

Dewitt Ranch Hotel Sign, 1972. Erie Boulevard through Dewitt developed in the 1960s as the county's quintessential automobile-based commercial strip. Like most across the country, it was garish and loud. Sign ordinances and continuing new construction have attempted to tone it down, but many fondly remember the lasso-twirling cowpoke and his diving girlfriend as the strip's most colorful landmark.

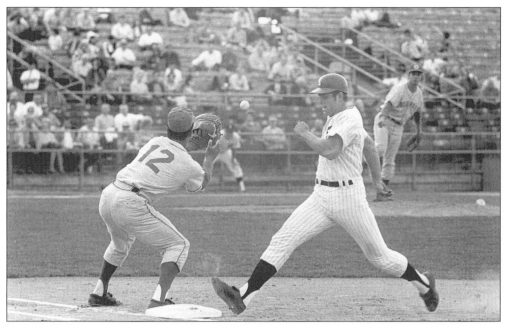

SYRACUSE CHIEFS AT BIG MAC, 1970. The International League Chiefs, now SkyChiefs, have been part of the county's heritage for most of the 20th century. Their home for the majority of it was MacArthur Stadium, replaced in 1997 by P&C Stadium.

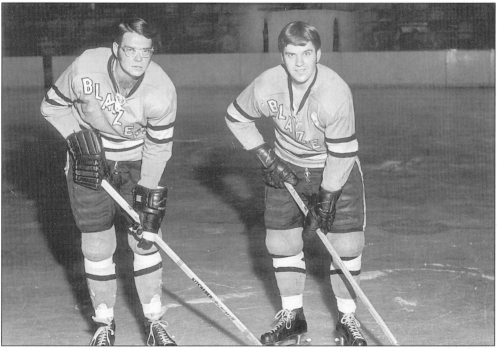

SYRACUSE BLAZERS BILL MCLEOD AND JIM WHITTAKER, 1970. Syracuse has been home to many professional hockey teams during the 20th century. The Crunch franchise, started here in 1994, will carry that banner into the 21st century, but for many Central New York fans, the rough and tumble Blazers of the 1967–76 period will always hold a fond place.

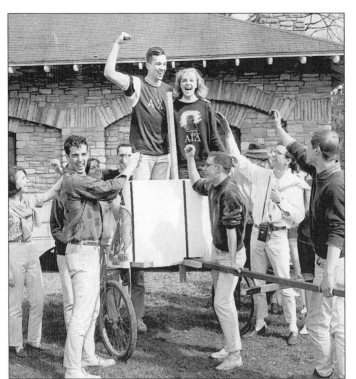

GREEK WEEK RACE AT THORNDEN PARK, 1965. This Hercules Chariot Race was just one of the spring social activities staged by the various campus fraternities and sororities in the mid-1960s.

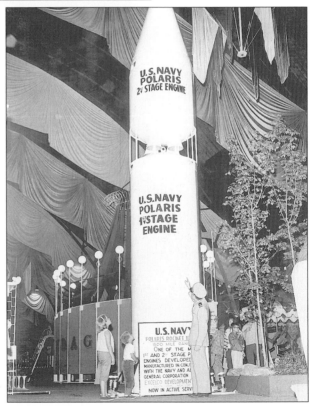

POLARIS MISSILE DISPLAY AT NEW YORK STATE FAIR, 1964. The 1950s and 1960s were the primary decades of the Cold War that pitted America against communism. An entire generation grew up with the lingering shadow of potential nuclear war. Patriotism was widespread and expected. Expressions of it appeared alongside the more carefree aspects of the annual fair.

104

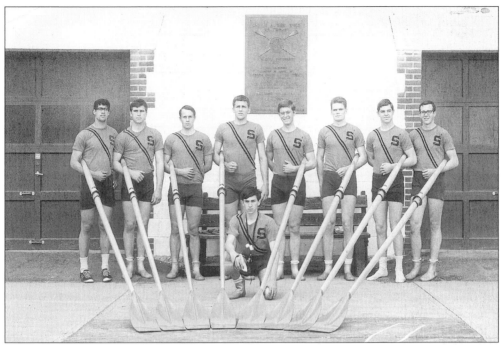

SYRACUSE UNIVERSITY VARSITY ROWING CREW, 1966. The annual Intercollegiate Rowing Association (IRA) Regatta on Onondaga Lake was a local spring tradition for 40 years, beginning in 1952.

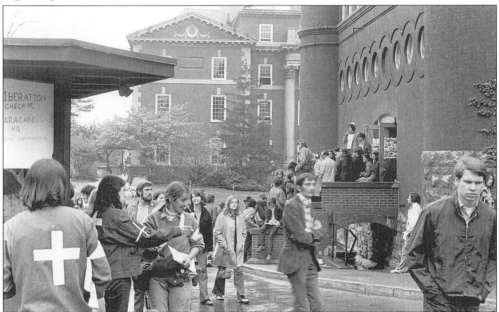

STUDENT OCCUPATION OF SYRACUSE UNIVERSITY ADMINISTRATION BUILDING, 1970. The escalating protests against the Vietnam War reached a crisis in the spring of 1970 when four students were shot by National Guardsmen at Kent State. S.U. students expressed their anger as well, giving the end of the 1960s a decidedly different feel on campus than its beginning. It would be another three years, however, before American troops were withdrawn from Vietnam.

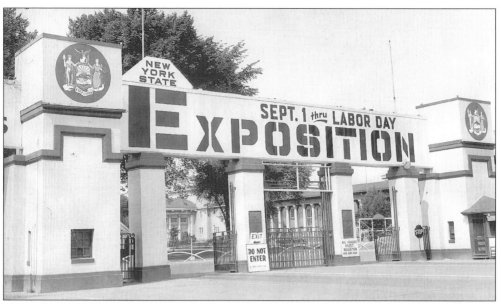

MAIN GATE AT NEW YORK STATE FAIR, 1964. The fair's entrance has undergone several versions over the years. This was its incarnation during the 1960s.

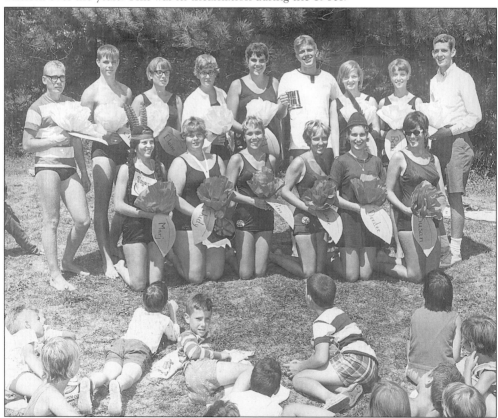

FAYETTEVILLE RECREATION SWIM STAFF AT GREEN LAKES, 1966. Instructors received gifts from the youngsters participating in an 8-week swim course.

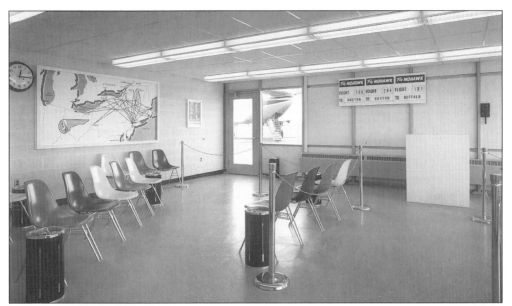

MOHAWK AIRLINES GATE AT HANCOCK AIRPORT, C. 1965. Before its merger into Allegheny Airlines in 1971, Mohawk was a small regional carrier serving the northeast United States. For a generation of Central New Yorkers, Mohawk provided their first flying experience.

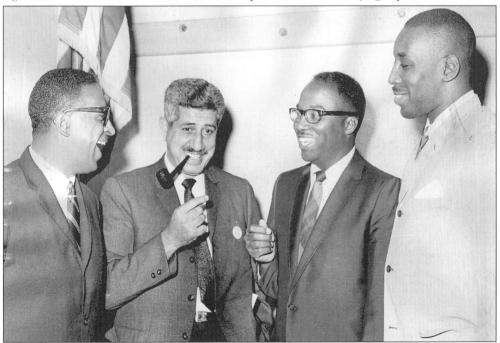

COMMUNITY LEADERS AT DUNBAR CENTER, 1968. Thanks to the efforts of the 1960s Civil Rights movement, and to leaders like these, issues of concern to African-Americans in Syracuse began to assume a larger profile in the community by the end of the decade. Shown here are, from left to right, as follows: Alfred Witcher, executive director of PEACE; Nicholas Rezak, associate executive director of Community Chest; Horace Ivey, president of Dunbar Center; and Emanuel Breland.

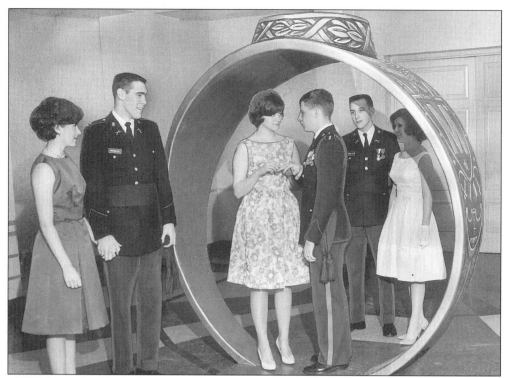

Manlius School Ring Dance, 1964. Here, cadets of the military academy receive rings from their dates in a traditional social event held at Knox Hall. The school would later become part of the present Manlius-Pebble Hill School in 1970, as interest waned in military careers.

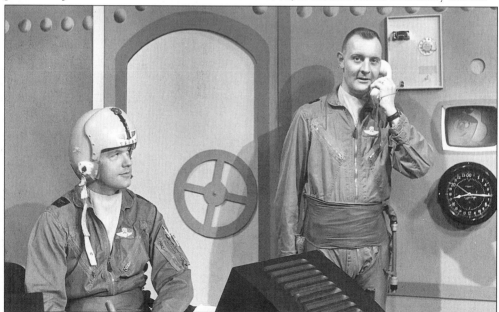

Jet Set TV Show, c. 1966. Inspired by NASA's then successful Gemini manned space program, local TV station WHEN developed this format with Colonel Skip and Colonel Joe hosting an afternoon children's cartoon program.

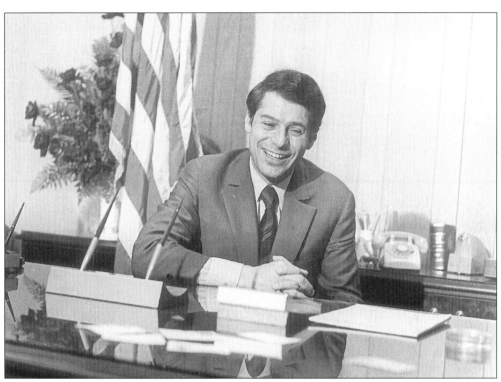

MAYOR LEE ALEXANDER, 1970.
Alexander had just won election to
his first term, and Syracuse looked
forward to a new era of growth
under this charismatic leader. He
became a powerful executive and
advanced many initiatives.
Alexander maintained his
popularity, winning reelection three
times, but ended his public life in
disgrace, pleading guilty to
extortion in 1988.

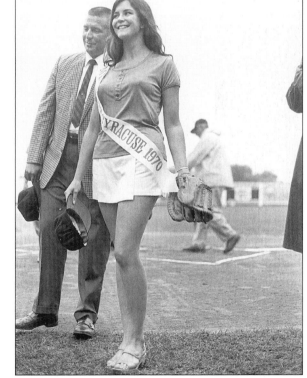

**OPENING PITCH AT MACARTHUR
STADIUM, 1970.** Miss North
Syracuse prepares to help the Chiefs
begin a new game. She also
demonstrates that the popular
miniskirt of the 1960s had climbed
to even newer heights by the start
of the 1970s.

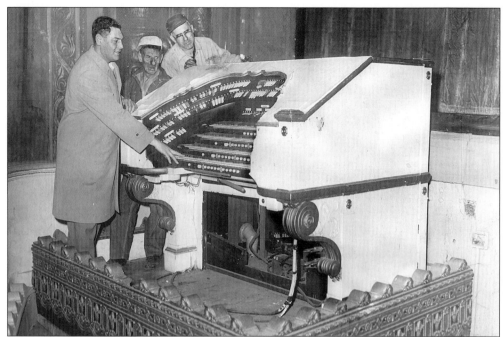

LOEW'S STATE THEATER ORGAN, 1965. This mighty Wurlitzer once entertained thousands of theater goers in the peak years of Syracuse's downtown movie palaces. Seen here, at the left, is Carston Henningsen of San Lorenzo, California. He bought and removed the organ in 1965, shipping it into storage on the west coast. Thirteen years later, when the theater was saved from demolition and earmarked for restoration, its loss was especially felt.

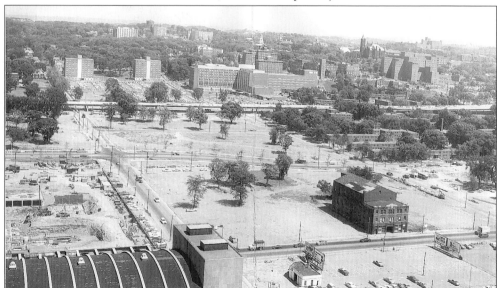

VIEW EAST FROM MONY TOWER, 1966. The effects of urban renewal can be seen here. An entire neighborhood has been eradicated southeast of downtown. Harrison Street (running from the foreground to the upper left) once was lined with small shops. Construction of the Everson Museum is visible (left). A few new office and apartment buildings were added subsequently, but the central block remains a parking lot as this is written.

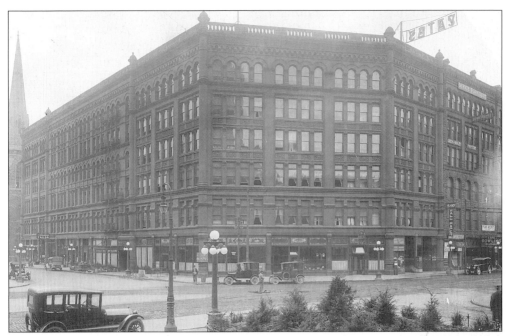

Yates Hotel at Montgomery and Washington Streets (Flashback to c. 1912). This grand building, designed by Archimedes Russell and opened in the 1890s, was a downtown landmark for 75 years. The Yates came down with the hope that the site could someday be redeveloped. Twenty-eight years later, it remains a parking lot.

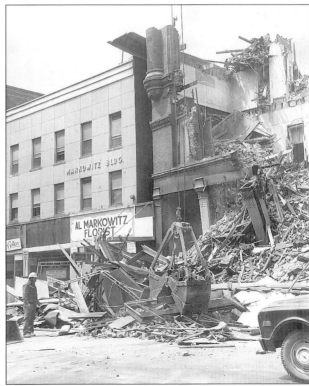

Yates Hotel Demolition, 1971. The belief that downtown needed to demolish old structures and modernize its look to compete with the suburbs held sway in the 1960s, 1970s, and even into the 1980s. Ironically, as the century drew to a close, it was the distinctive historic character of districts like Syracuse's Armory Square that have proven to be key toward revitalization of many older downtowns.

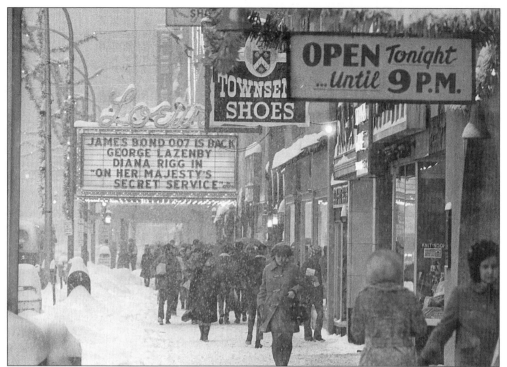

ALONG THE 300 BLOCK OF SOUTH SALINA STREET, 1969. Winter weather is a permanent part of the local scene. The blizzard of 1966 is most often spoke of as the worst local residents had to endure, at least in the second half of the century. For these shoppers, the winter landscape on this day is merely typical.

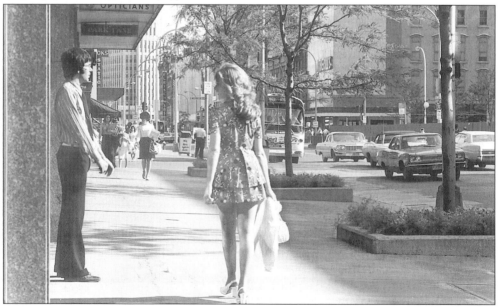

ALONG THE 100 BLOCK OF SOUTH SALINA STREET, C. 1973. The community had changed and experienced much after nearly three quarters of the century had passed. Compare this scene to that on page 15.

Six
1975–1999

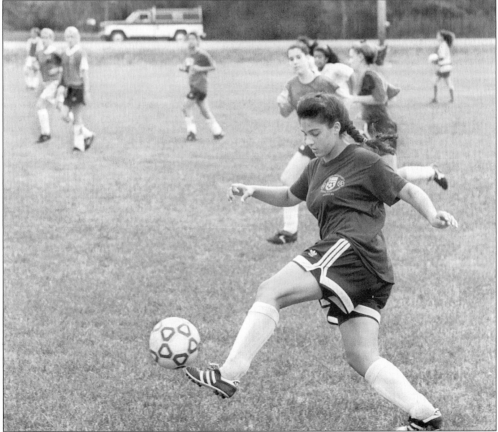

LIVERPOOL HIGH SCHOOL SOCCER PRACTICE, 1991. One can discover a wide variety of sports played in Central New York throughout the 20th century. For its last quarter, however, soccer has enjoyed a distinctive surge in popularity, particularly among area youth. Here, Liverpool player Laurie Yacovella moves the ball down field.

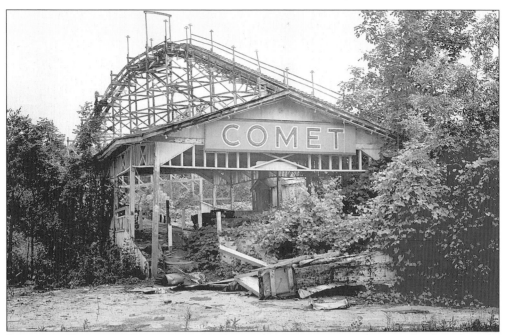

SUBURBAN PARK IN MANLIUS, 1975. This modest amusement park was a familiar place for generations of Central New Yorkers to enjoy the summer months. By 1975, it closed. The land was eventually developed for housing and offices.

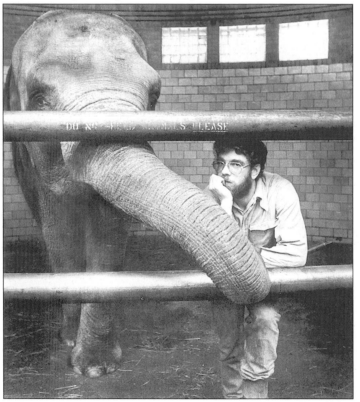

SIRI AND CHUCK DOYLE AT BURNET PARK ZOO, 1980. By the 1980s, Syracuse's old city zoo facility had become severely antiquated. As community leaders debated whether to renovate or abandon it for a new facility, its resident Asian elephant, Siri, became a symbol of the problem when she outgrew her cramped quarters. Renovation was chosen and the new Burnet Park Zoo opened in 1986.

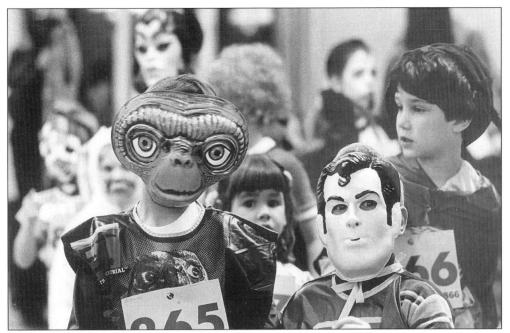

E.T. AND SUPERMAN, C. 1983. Actually, these are children at a Halloween party at Andrews Memorial Methodist Church in North Syracuse. Superman, while a popular cultural figure for decades, was rediscovered by a new generation when a big-budget Superman movie was released in 1978. E.T., the extra-terrestrial, became a brand new icon of the era with the release of that enormously popular science fiction feature in 1982.

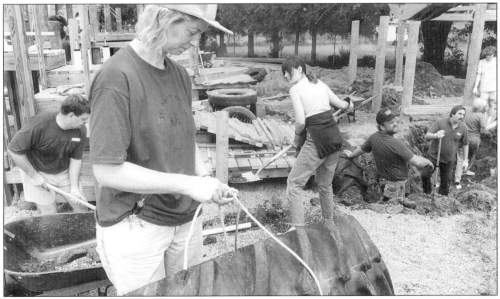

VOLUNTEERS CONSTRUCT PLAYGROUND IN TULLY, 1992. The final decades of the 20th century witnessed a growing realization that government could not afford to meet all the interests of an increasingly diverse citizenry. Volunteer groups sometimes stepped forward to help insure that non-mandated offerings could be realized. Here, parents literally help build a playground behind Tully Elementary School.

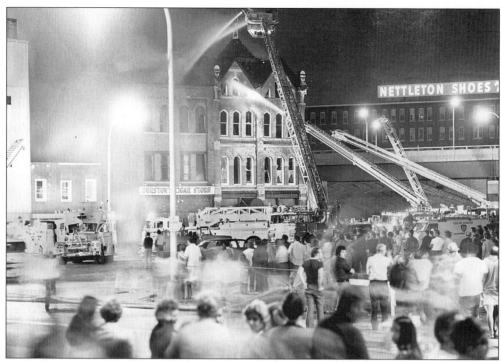

EXPLOSION AND FIRE AT NORTH SALINA AND WILLOW STREETS, 1975. One of the more dramatic downtown fires of the last quarter century occurred in the summer of 1975, when arson destroyed Besdin's, a large furniture store. Most of the crowd was drawn to the drama of whether firefighters could save the nearby Colella Antique Galleries (center), a renovated 1879 landmark. They did.

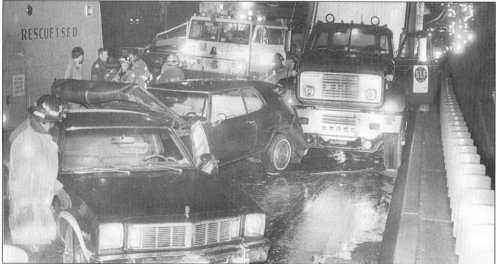

ROUTE 81 ACCIDENT NEAR PEARL STREET ENTRANCE, 1982. The expressways and highways that were developed by the 1960s and 1970s around Syracuse helped expedite traffic, but their high speeds, combined with Central New York's fickle weather, meant drivers needed to be extra cautious. Route 81 has been the scene of some dramatic pileups in the last quarter of this century.

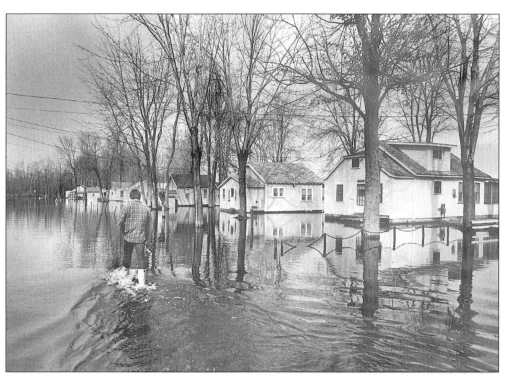

BEACH ROAD IN CICERO, 1981. Stretches of Oneida Lake's south shore were opened in the post–World War II years for the construction of summer "camps." Oneida Lake water levels, regulated as part of the New York State Barge Canal system, sometimes experience problems in times of heavy rains and spring runoff (as seen above).

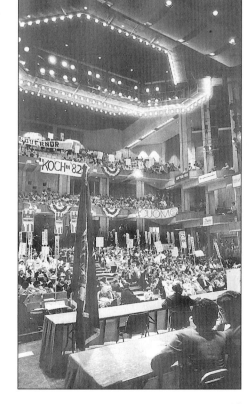

DEMOCRATIC STATE CONVENTION AT CIVIC CENTER, 1982. The center's Crouse-Hinds Theater was the scene of a spirited contest for the Democratic nomination for governor between supporters of New York City Mayor Ed Koch and State official Mario Cuomo. Koch won but was subsequently beat by Cuomo in the primary. Cuomo went on to three terms as governor.

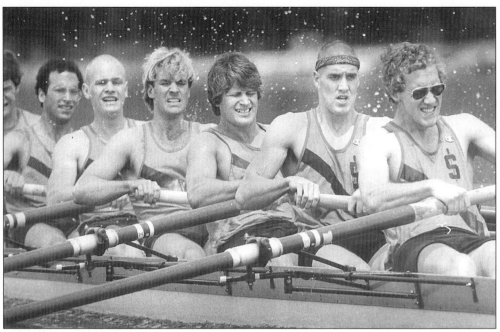

SYRACUSE UNIVERSITY VARSITY CREW CAPTURING PACKARD CUP ON ONONDAGA LAKE, 1983. Throughout the 20th century, the waters of Onondaga Lake have played host to thousands of "heats," featuring some of the best collegiate rowers in the country. The most famous series, the IRA Regatta, was based here from 1952 until 1992.

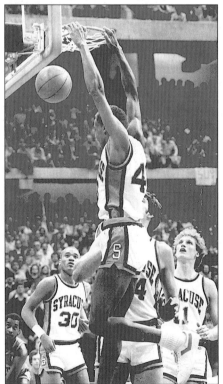

S.U. BASKETBALL, 1981. Syracuse University basketball enjoyed new popularity during the 1980s and 1990s, with the team reaching the NCAA final championship game twice. The completion of S.U.'s domed stadium in 1980 gave them one of the largest collegiate basketball venues in the nation. Here, Erich Santifer completes a classic dunk.

LOCAL SOFTBALL PLAY, 1982. The last quarter of the 20th century saw a growing effort to place women in sports on an equal footing with their male counterparts. This occurred in organized team play at various school levels, increasingly in the professional sphere, and even with the increase of mixed coed softball leagues during the 1980s.

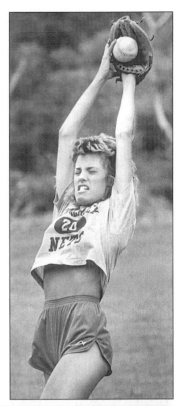

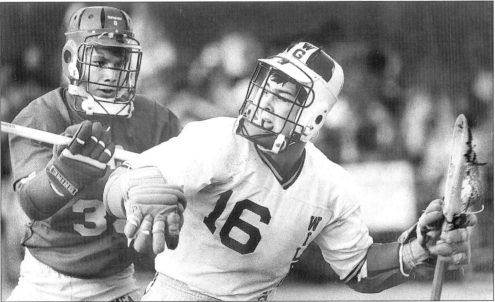

STATE CHAMPIONSHIP LACROSSE PLAYOFFS, 1983. Lacrosse, a traditional Iroquois game, is probably the oldest local sporting activity. It enjoyed a widespread resurgence during the final quarter of the 20th century. During this period, West Genesee High School amassed a stunning record of victories, including this game against Ithaca, which featured #16, attacker Todd Curry.

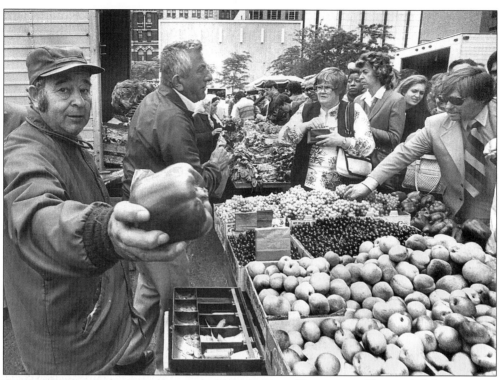

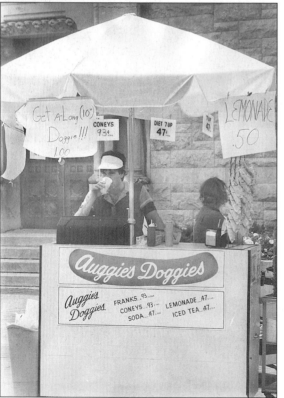

DOWNTOWN FARMER'S MARKET, 1980. The flight of retail to the suburbs during the later part of the 20th century has caused downtown Syracuse to seek different approaches for maintaining the vitality of the central core. Returning a regular summer market to downtown has been one successful approach. A farmer's market also occupied Clinton Square at the 20th century's start.

COLUMBUS CIRCLE HOT DOG STAND, 1982. Vendor carts became a new and initially controversial feature of downtown during the 1970s and 1980s. Restaurant owners were concerned with the competition, and others worried about the unkempt appearance of some carts. City regulations eventually addressed these issues to some degree.

SHOPPINGTOWN MALL, 1991. The shopping plaza building boom of the 1950s was followed in the 1970s and 1980s by the arrival of the enclosed retail mall. Some original plazas, like Shoppingtown, were converted into malls to maintain their competitive edge.

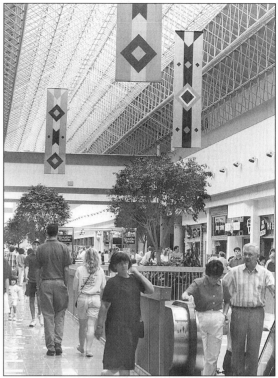

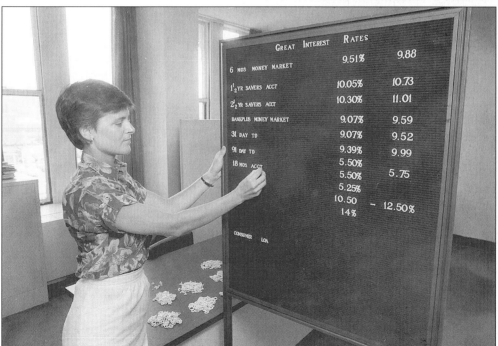

GREAT INTEREST RATES		
6 MOS MONEY MARKET	9.51%	9.88
1½ YR SAVERS ACCT	10.05%	10.73
2½ YR SAVERS ACCT	10.30%	11.01
BANKPLUS MONEY MARKET	9.07%	9.59
31 DAY TD	9.07%	9.52
91 DAY TD	9.39%	9.99
18 MOS ACCT	5.50%	
	5.50%	5.75
	5.25%	
	10.50	12.50%
	14%	
CONSUMER LOA		

SYRACUSE SAVINGS BANK, 1983. The interest rates for savings accounts in the inflation-driven years of the early 1980s seem impressively high, 16 years later, at the end of the 20th century.

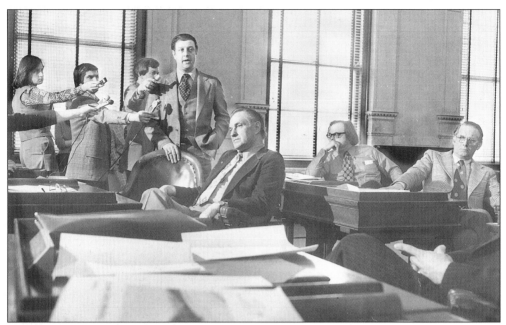

MICHAEL J. BRAGMAN AND COUNTY LEGISLATORS, 1977. Local voters gained familiarity with Bragman during his years as Democratic leader in the county legislature. It served as a departure point to run for the state assembly in 1980. His success there has brought him to the post of assembly majority leader, where he has been able to assist with many Central New York projects.

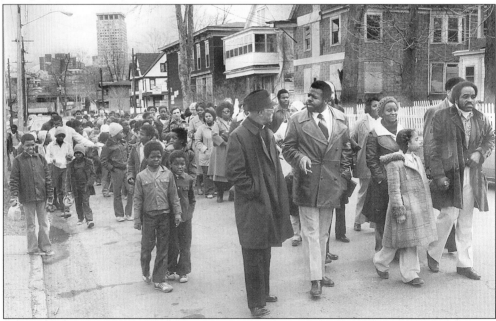

MARTIN LUTHER KING JR. COMMEMORATIVE MARCH, 1979. Local NAACP president, Reverend Emory Proctor (left), and past president, Reverend John D. Jones (right), lead marchers from the city elementary school on Castle Street named for the slain civil rights leader.

WOMAN CONSTRUCTION WORKER, 1983. The women's rights movement that arose during the social unrest of the 1960s continued throughout the remainder of the 20th century, attempting to break down both laws and traditions that held women back in many fields. One could see the results increasingly taking hold during the late 20th century in various traditionally male occupations such as the construction trades.

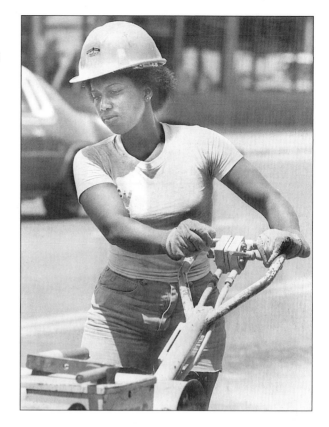

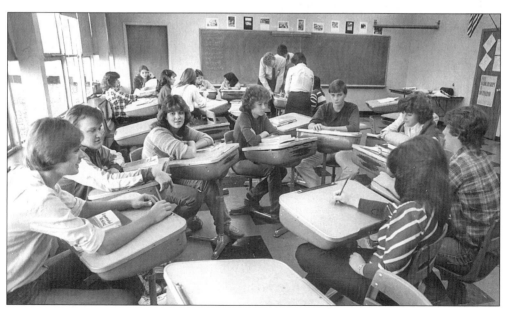

JOURNALISM CLASS AT WEST GENESEE HIGH SCHOOL, 1982. Classroom education assumed a more informal look by the late 1970s.

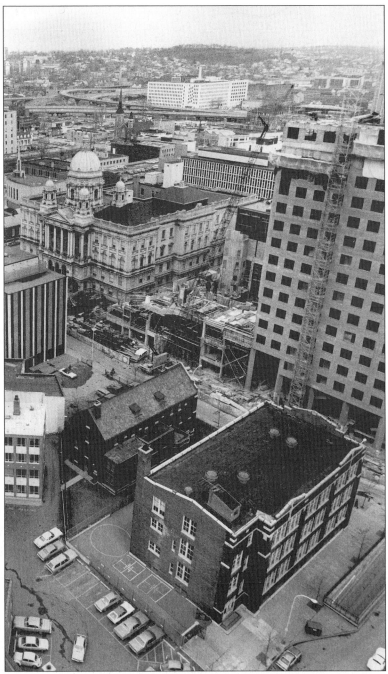

CONSTRUCTION OF THE CIVIC CENTER, 1975. County executive John Mulroy, in a innovative move, linked the need for additional government office space with the dream of local arts advocates for a multi-purpose theater complex. The result was the county facility that came to bear his name. Like the opening of the new Everson Museum of Art in the previous decade, this performing arts complex helped Syracuse and Onondaga County maintain a quality of life quotient that has become essential in the late 20th century for maintaining an attractive and competitive community.

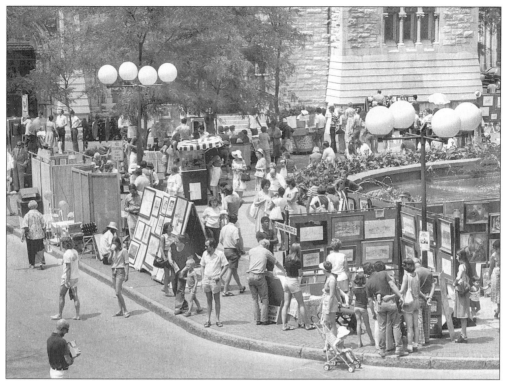

ARTS & CRAFTS FESTIVAL IN COLUMBUS CIRCLE, 1978. Started in the early 1970s, this event has become one of downtown Syracuse's most successful annual events. It draws a diverse crowd and helps focus attention on downtown and its attractions. It has continued for nearly 30 years.

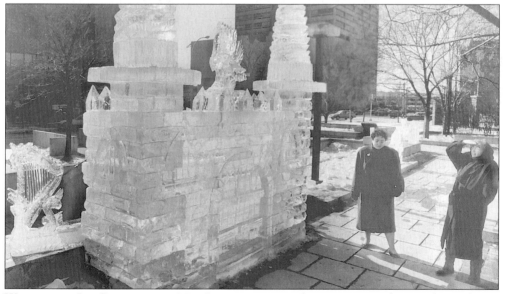

WINTERFEST ICE SCULPTURE, 1992. In a community where winter weather can linger for six months, it seemed natural to launch a winterfest for Syracuse in the 1980s. Ironically, the event was periodically plagued with streaks of unusually warm temperatures. The annual event has continued but never achieved the scale once anticipated.

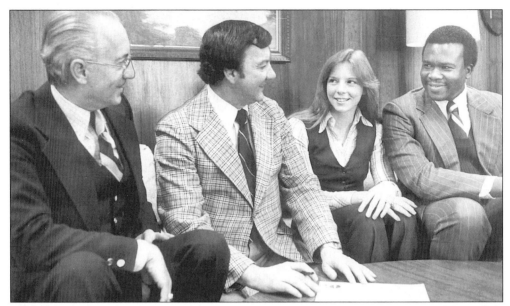

John Mulroy and Junior Achievement Officials, 1978. Mulroy, second from left, became the county's first executive in 1962, a new position created in a reorganization of the county charter. Mulroy led county government for 26 years and raised its profile considerably as new community-wide issues surfaced that could only be successfully addressed with the strength of county-wide resources.

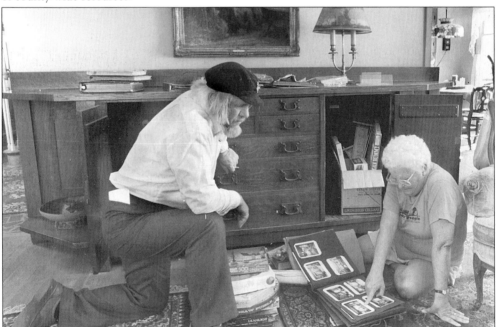

Peter and Harriet Wiles, 1988. Peter Wiles led efforts in the 1970s and 1980s to increase use and appreciation of the state's canal waterways. He also was the grandson of mission furniture innovator Gustav Stickley. In 1988, he sent this sideboard and other personal Stickley pieces to auction. Estimated to bring as much as $80,000, this piece was purchased by Barbra Streisand for a record $363,000!

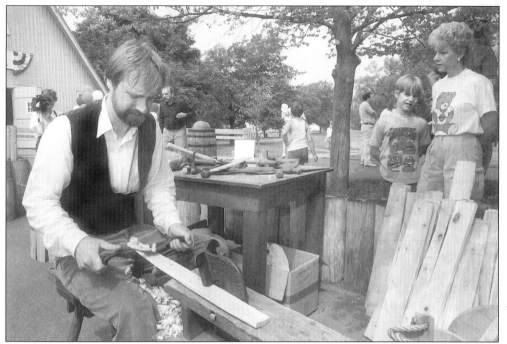

COOPERING DEMONSTRATION AT SALT MUSEUM, 1991. This museum of local salt history and the nearby re-creation of colonial Saint Marie, both built in 1933, experienced a rejuvenation in the late 1970s and 1980s. Onondaga County Parks created a professional museum office and increased appropriations. The result was a new appreciation for two of the richest portions of this community's heritage. Here George Pobedinsky works on a shaving bench.

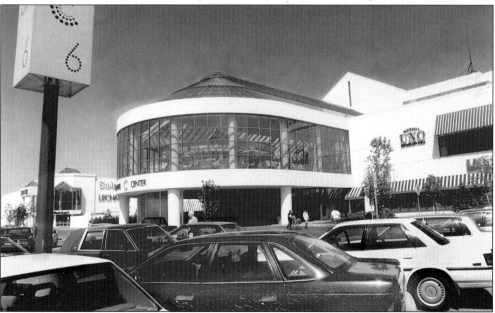

CAROUSEL CENTER MALL, 1992. The 1990 opening of the massive Carousel Mall, on the south shore of Onondaga Lake, redefined the local retail scene and, as the 21st century approached, set the stage for revitalizing Syracuse's lake front.

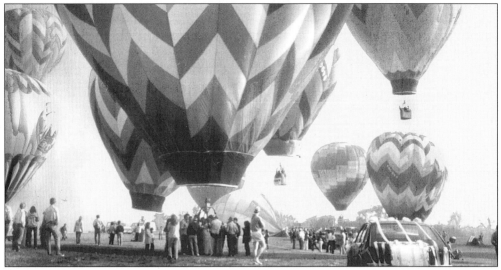

BALLOON FESTIVAL AT JAMESVILLE BEACH, 1982. For the 1980s and 1990s, this June event has helped mark the start of the summer season. Dozens of colorful balloons make their ascent, framed by the green hills of Pompey and underlined by the blue waters of the Jamesville Reservoir. Hot air balloon launches have filled and always will fill people with wonder, no matter what the century.

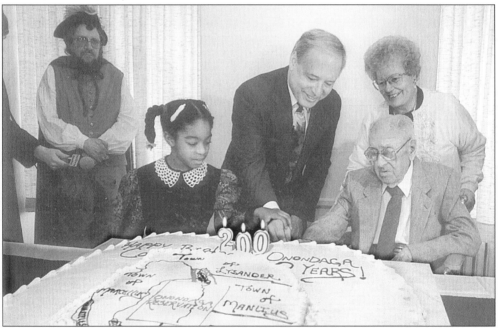

ONONDAGA COUNTY'S BICENTENNIAL CAKE CUTTING AT THE OHA MUSEUM, 1994. The 20th century's last decade included the 200th anniversary of Onondaga County's formation. Ed Sauer, a centenarian who was a young child when the county turned 100 in 1894, was on hand to cut the cake with county executive Nick Pirro and Aisha Mitchell. Mitchell represented the youth that will inherit the leadership of this community in the next century, one that will undoubtedly witness changes even more amazing than those spread across the time span of Ed Sauer's life.